How the Fed Moves Markets

How the Fed Moves Markets

Central Bank Analysis for the Modern Era

Evan A. Schnidman and William D. MacMillan

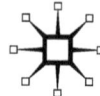

HOW THE FED MOVES MARKETS
Copyright © Evan A. Schnidman and William D. MacMillan 2016

All rights reserved. No reproduction, copy or transmission of this publication may be made without written permission. No portion of this publication may be reproduced, copied or transmitted save with written permission. In accordance with the provisions of the Copyright, Designs and Patents Act 1988, or under the terms of any licence permitting limited copying issued by the Copyright Licensing Agency, Saffron House, 6-10 Kirby Street, London EC1N 8TS.

Any person who does any unauthorized act in relation to this publication may be liable to criminal prosecution and civil claims for damages.

First published 2016 by
PALGRAVE MACMILLAN

The authors have asserted their rights to be identified as the authors of this work in accordance with the Copyright, Designs and Patents Act 1988.

Palgrave Macmillan in the UK is an imprint of Macmillan Publishers Limited, registered in England, company number 785998, of Houndmills, Basingstoke, Hampshire, RG21 6XS.

Palgrave Macmillan in the US is a division of Nature America, Inc., One New York Plaza, Suite 4500, New York, NY 10004-1562.

Palgrave Macmillan is the global academic imprint of the above companies and has companies and representatives throughout the world.

Hardback ISBN: 978–1–137–43257–5
E-PUB ISBN: 978–1–137–43259–9
E-PDF ISBN: 978–1–137–43258–2
DOI: 10.1057/9781137432582

Distribution in the UK, Europe and the rest of the world is by Palgrave Macmillan®, a division of Macmillan Publishers Limited, registered in England, company number 785998, of Houndmills, Basingstoke, Hampshire RG21 6XS.

Library of Congress Cataloging-in-Publication Data is available from the Library of Congress.

A catalogue record for the book is available from the British Library.

Contents

List of Figures and Tables   vii

Foreword   ix

Introduction   1

PART I   Emergence and Evolution: The Story of the Fed

1. Origins: From Chaos to Structure   9
2. Independence: Wars, Depression, and Politics   17
3. Centralization: The Rise of Technocracy   31
4. Transparency: Data Meets Democracy   39

PART II   Fed Watching: Sentiment Analysis and Data-Driven Investing

5. The Briefcase Watch: Fed Watching at Its Finest?   51
6. Data-Driven Fed Watching: Comprehensive, Unbiased, and Quantitative   59
7. Fixed-Income Investing: Fed Sentiment Drives Bonds   69
8. Equity Market Investing: Macro Matters   79
9. Forecasting Policy: Market Response to Fed Communication Trends   89
10. FOREX Investing: Central Bank Sentiment Data across the Globe   99

PART III   Global Monetary Policy: Analyzing Central Banks around the World

11. ECB Sentiment: Decoding a Complex Monetary Union   115

12 BOE Sentiment: The Origin of Modern Central Bank Communications   127
13 BOJ Sentiment: Monetary Clues in Lost Decades   137
14 RBA Sentiment: Australia as a Proxy for China   147
15 Global Sentiment: International Central Bank Transparency   159

Conclusion   183

Bibliography   189

Index   197

Figures and Tables

Figures

1.1	Twelve Federal Reserve district boundaries as they were drawn by the RBOC	12
7.1	Performance of a Fed Index-driven simulated portfolio	75
7.2	Fed Index, FFR, and a ten-year bond yield	76
8.1	Fed Index, Russell 2K, S&P 500, and NASDAQ from 1997 to 2014	85
8.2	Correlation of Fed Index with standard market indexes	86
8.3	Correlation of Fed Index with industrial sector indexes	86
8.4	Fed Index-driven simulated stock portfolio value, compared to major indexes	87
9.1	FOMC meetings forecast, one-week lag	93
9.2	Fed Index six-month moving average, April–September 2013	94
9.3	Fed Index projection as of December 14, 2013, and actual FOMC sentiment	95
9.4	Fed Index-led portfolio, the S&P 500, and the Dow Jones	97
10.1	USD-basket of currencies with Fed Index	103
10.2	ECB-USD with bank trends	104
10.3	GBP-USD with bank trends	105
10.4	JPY-USD with bank trends	106
10.5	CAD-USD with bank trends	107
10.6	AUD-CNY with bank trends	108
10.7	AUD-USD with bank trends	108
11.1	ECB Index and the ECB ten-year bond yield	123

11.2	ECB Index and European equities indexes	124
12.1	BOE Index, FTSE 100, and NASDAQ	133
12.2	BOE Index portfolio against buy-and-hold	135
13.1	BOJ Index and the Nikkei 225	142
13.2	BOJ Index and Japanese government ten-year bond yield	143
13.3	BOJ Index, yen-USD, and yen-euro	145
14.1	RBA Index, the ASX 500, and SSE Composite Index	151
14.2	RBA Index and Australian government ten-year bond yield	153
14.3	RBA Index and Chinese benchmarks	153
14.4	AUD-CNY and RBA Index	155
14.5	AUD-CNY and RBA Index (less smoothed)	156
15.1	BOC Index and TSX 60	161
15.2	SWE Index and OMX 30	163
15.3	SWE Index and Swedish government ten-year bond yield	163
15.4	RNZ Index and exchange rates	165
15.5	SNB Index and Swiss Market Index (SMI)	167
15.6	BOK Index and KRX 100	169
15.7	BOI Index and Israeli government ten-year bond yield	171
15.8	BOM Index and Mexican IPC	173
15.9	BCB Index and the BM&F BOVESPA Index	175
15.10	CBR Index and the MICEX Index	177
15.11	RBI Index and exchange rates	178
15.12	SARB Index and FTSE/JSE 40	180

Tables

1.1	Federal Reserve district populations in 1913 and 2000	13
3.1	Regional Bank president backgrounds	36

Foreword

This book was first conceived while reading a newspaper in early 2008 before the financial crisis, before the world knew terms like "quantitative easing," "tapering," and "considerable time." In fact, the spark for this book occurred before the Fed chair began holding regularly scheduled press conferences or the Fed even adopted an explicit inflation target. When I first conceived of this subject, all I knew was that Fed policy was confusing and the focus on few singular words seemed to be causing market turmoil as the housing crisis became a financial crisis—and nearly a financial panic.

After that fateful day reading a newspaper as a college student in early 2008, I set out to organize my graduate school curriculum around researching central banks. I studied their origins, politics, policy, evolution, and most importantly, their communications. What I found was astounding: over the last two decades central banks have become more transparent than at any point in their history, but the modern methods of "Fed watching" have not kept pace with this change in central bank communication. In fact, modern Fed watching often looks like a glorified version of the "Briefcase Watch" from the early 1990s. The big difference is that today Fed watchers are not cuing in on the thickness of Alan Greenspan's briefcase; rather they are hanging on singular words from Janet Yellen. This focus on single words or phrases lends itself to groupthink and negates the careful construction of whole central bank communications, thus leaving vital information about policy unanalyzed. This book, and the methodology presented here, is the first attempt to solve that problem with comprehensive, unbiased, quantitative central bank sentiment data.

Our data has been jointly developed by myself and my coauthor William MacMillan, but we would be remiss if we did not extend our deepest gratitude to several others who have made our data development, business development, and the writing of this book possible. First and foremost are our families: both Bill and I walked away from the calmer academic lifestyle in favor of the constant pressure of entrepreneurship; the people bearing the brunt of that pressure are our respective families, particularly our wives, Jacque MacMillan and Whitney Phipps. Thank you for putting up with the long hours, incessant travel, constant aggravation, and general stress. We truly appreciate it.

Along with the strain on our family and friends, this book would never have been possible if it was not for our incredible staff. Natty Hoffman has done a masterful job picking up operational slack while I have been busy with this book project. Similarly, Jermell Beane has been invaluable in his work building and maintaining our data management systems. In this process, our data development team has been transformed to an army of researchers and we are deeply grateful to Alister Bent, William Stein, Halle Orr, and Michelle Tuma. Worthy of particular mention is our senior researcher, Joe Sutherland, who has demonstrated himself to not only be an extraordinarily hard worker, but a brilliant researcher as well.

Finally, this book would never have been possible without Alex Detmering. Alex is not only our director of content at Prattle, he is also our technical writer, editor, researcher, thought-organizer, and the manager who pulled this all together. Like Bill and I, Alex has subjected his family and friends to the strains of this process, so we would like to extend a particular thanks to Stephen Fairbanks who provided editorial support to Alex and therefore to us. We would also like to thank Sarah Detmering, Alex's wife, for tolerating the long hours of work Alex has put into this project.

As I am sure any reader has by now surmised, this book has truly been a collaborative effort to share Bill's and my research with the world. We hope that this work not only clearly explains our new method of analyzing central banks, but it also gets you thinking about how to use fundamental economic data (like central bank policy) to make sound investment decisions. We believe understanding central bank communications (and therefore policy) is crucial to any investment strategy; it is our sincere hope that the methodology and data presented in the book help others to understand central banks better than they ever have before.

Introduction

Like many Federal buildings, it's very square. Very flat. Very square. Four flat, square pillars frame the entrance to the building, which is almost entirely white. The entrance is embedded in a massive, alabaster cube—the head of the imposing structure—and, extending out from its level left and right cheeks, are two long, identical, rectangular buildings. These too would be completely white if it weren't for the tall, black strips dedicated to office windows that run the length of each with perfect symmetry. Flanked by two square, carefully curated lawns, a narrow path, deep gray and direct, runs from the small steps at the edge of the property to the entrance. Bare of almost any ornament, the architecture's lone flourish is the bone-white statue of an eagle that sits directly above its front door, overseeing the strict geometry and bleached colors of the Eccles Building, headquarters of the Federal Reserve.

Banks look like temples. Not every bank, obviously, but many do. The Eccles Building certainly does, and it doesn't require too much to understand why. The stone pillars, the clean architecture, and the symmetry, all the features of the bank's striking exterior impart the highest degree of sobriety and seriousness—of trust. Above all, trust is essential for the financial system, and nowhere is this necessity more evident than it is with money.

In a very real sense, money is a measure of trust. For instance, the faith American citizens have in their federal government sustains the value of their currency. And what is true of currency is also very true of the institutions that process it—banks. Like currency, banks succeed or fail based on the trust that they can inspire. For instance, it is a well-known fact that banks continually operate with reserves that do not match the total amount their customers could withdraw. This practice, known as fractional reserve banking, is fundamental to banking operations and is also demonstrative of the integral part trust plays in the financial system. While any given bank could not possibly withstand the simultaneous full withdrawal of all its demand deposit accounts, we trust that when we need it, the money will be available.

But, with the Eccles Building, with the Federal Reserve, the temple comparison runs deeper. The design invokes more than trust. With exquisite precision, emerald lawns and ivory masonry grant an aura of sacred—almost divine—authority, and, given its charge, the appearance is fitting. With over a thousand economists at hand and the printing press of the Treasury on tap, the Federal Reserve is the financial vatican—an institution whose powers and prestige have only grown over the hundred-plus years since its founding. This ascendancy has been particularly evident since the financial crisis, where unprecedented Fed policies, like quantitative easing, have grabbed center stage in an economy reeling from the fallout of the housing market's collapse. During this period of global instability, the Fed has emerged as the undisputed leader—a commanding position the central bank seems well suited for.

The power that the Fed wields extends to its words, which have, just like the rest of the central bank's tools, multiplied in recent years. In the entire history of the Federal Reserve, the institution has never been more verbose, never been more transparent. Communication has become an integral tool of monetary policy, used not only to explain policy—but actually as policy. Put plainly, the Fed's words move markets and have, therefore, become a vital source of economic influence for the institution. It is this development and the market practices that have developed in response that are the central narrative of this book.

* * *

It wasn't too long ago that the Fed's version of transparency was briefcase. In the early 1990s, the width of Alan Greenspan's briefcase was one of the sparse bits of evidence that financial analysts—now known as Fed watchers—had to go on to project the central bank's ensuing monetary policy actions. The theory was as follows: a thick briefcase meant that Greenspan has been reviewing numbers and was likely to make change in monetary policy; a thin briefcase carried the opposite implication. Interestingly, although the Federal

Reserve's communicative practices have certainly changed, the interpretive methods fundamental to the "briefcase watch" haven't quite as much.

Despite the fact that the Fed, among other things, now releases meeting minutes and holds press conferences, Fed watchers often give an inordinate amount of attention to the granular details of the central bank's communications to make their projections. This approach does seem appropriate for the interpretation of press releases that the Fed updates through track changes, but its application has extended to the full breadth of the text now available over the multiple channels the central bank utilizes to communicate their message. By focusing on individual words and phrases instead of attending to the entire text—let alone the broad trends that arise when taking into account all the central bank's channels—modern Fed watchers are functionally performing an interpretive method comparable to those that powered the "briefcase watch": using minute details to back bold forecasts. This myopic approach is clearly vulnerable to miscalculation—section bias being but one of the myriad of potential errors that could contaminate analysis.

In the modern market, the evaluation of Federal Reserve's communications is simply too important to be functionally monopolized by such methods. Realizing this, we have developed a system of textual interpretation specifically calibrated to tackle central bank texts. Current methods rely on individual interpretation of particular details to produce qualitative interpretations of the Fed's current economic position and projections of the central bank's future policy moves. Built on the breadth of historical connections between the Fed's words and the market's reactions, our methodology generates a quantitative analysis of the entire bandwidth of Fed communications released within a given time period. This data, known as the Prattle Sentiment Index, represents the first comprehensive, real-time, unbiased, and quantitative interpretations of Federal Reserve communications in existence.

* * *

This book is divided into three parts. The first part is dedicated to the birth and evolution of the modern Fed—tracing the gradual development of the institution's utilization of transparency.

Growing out of a troubled banking system and chronic economic collapses, the Federal Reserve was created to serve as the financial backbone of the nation. Under this charge, the Fed and its specific powers and privileges would continuously evolve over a series of monumental challenges—trials that began with the Great Depression. Not even 20 years after its inception, the young central bank was first confronted with an economy in ashes—then a world at war. This global conflict was quickly followed by the Korean War and the stagflation crisis. As the Fed reacted to each wave of chaos, changes began to brew. The institution began to grow more academic to deal with the tremendous complexity of the problems it faced; it grew more centralized to create the stability and power needed to act; it grew more independent to give itself the freedom to act according to the data-driven recommendations of its expert personnel. As the Fed became more centralized, autonomous, and technocratic, those outside the institution looked on—with anxiety—at a financial fortress. It became apparent the Fed's power needed to be balanced with openness—with transparency. The culmination of that development is the purview of the book's second part.

Focusing on the era of the transparent Federal Reserve, Part II chronicles how "Fedspeak" changed from a tool of obfuscation to means of open communication—and what that evolution meant (and means) for the market. Fed Chairmen Paul Volcker and Alan Greenspan were famous for using obscure and opaque verbiage to comment on Fed's position. This rhetorical technique, known as Fedspeak, was meant to maintain a veil of mystery around the central bank, keeping its intentions unknown and unknowable. By the close of Greenspan's tenure, Fedspeak began to take on an entirely different role: clarification. Bernanke and Yellen have continued this trend, harnessing communication to calm markets and explain policy. As the Fed embraced transparency, an analytic tradition grew, and our methodology was born of frustration with these orthodox methods. Exploring the mechanics of our process, this part looks at how our data performs in the equity, fixed-income, and FOREX markets and puts both our methodology and the thesis that the Fed's words move markets to the test.

The third part looks at transparency as a global phenomenon. While the Fed and its practices may be the focus of this book, open communication is far from a local development. The European Central Bank, the Bank of England, the Bank of Japan and many other central banks around the world have also integrated transparency as a vital tool of monetary policy, and our methodology also applies to those banks. As the previous part did with the Fed, Part III investigates how our data on these central banks bears out against market oscillations.

* * *

Over the past decade, the economic landscape has changed dramatically. The titanic sums that flow through the financial markets have increasingly been shepherded by the hand of central bankers. For financial professionals, these developments make grappling with the impact central banks have on the economy more vital than ever before—and integral to that effort is the study of the effects of central banking communications. These texts stand as perhaps the most unwieldy aspect of central banking policy, and, in both academia and the private sector, the impact they have on the market is only beginning to be examined. Our work in this space has afforded us the ability to take a unique look at the authority and power central banks command and, through our novel approach, better understand the institutions that govern the financial world.

PART I

Emergence and Evolution: The Story of the Fed

1

Origins: From Chaos to Structure

Even a century after its founding, the US Federal Reserve remains an enigma in the minds of many Americans. Scholars have spent decades examining the inner workings and evolution of powers exercised by Congress, the presidency, the bureaucracy, and the courts, but, despite the tremendous power the Fed wields, its history and mechanics are seldom researched, let alone understood. The next few chapters will explore the history of banking's ultimate black box, a history inundated with not only, of course, board meetings and bureaucracy, but also political intrigue, power plays, pioneers, and traitors. Amid warring factions and economic disasters, the last century has seen the Fed evolve dramatically. Originally designed as a regional organism, the Fed in the twenty-first century is a centralized machine of information aggregation. At its inception, its policy emerged from a plurality of voices; now that policy is the product of complex data analyses and processes. The Fed has transformed, in other words, from democracy to data.

The Fed has also, and perhaps most importantly, become increasingly independent—an independence it secures through an open communications policy. This transparency, now known as forward guidance, has not only become a vital aspect of policy—it is policy (Yellen 2012). Fundamental to an adequate understanding of the Fed, transparency is central to this book, and its development is an essential theme in the Fed's history.

Centralized, technocratic, independent, and transparent—although technically the same institution, the modern central bank is very different from the institution as it was first designed in 1913. The modern institution, however, cannot be properly understood without first looking at its origins.

* * *

The late nineteenth century was a most volatile time in America's financial history. Riddled with financial panics and crises that struck almost every decade between the American Civil War and World War I, the US economy reeled under a nationally chartered private banking system that followed the "Free Bank Era" (1837–1862). In *Yankee Leviathan*, Cornell scholar Richard Bensel identifies a dysfunctional US Treasury as the source of the turmoil. The rise of finance and capitalists in a single-party system in the North bred clientelism and corruption sustained by finance-obsessed political appointees dogmatically opposed to state intervention in the economy. These Treasury positions limited "radical reconstruction" efforts—such as wealth redistribution—and placed the US economy back on the gold standard in an effort to resume international trade. Treasury actions, according to Bensel, not only limited reconstruction efforts, but also fueled the banking panics that culminated in the panic of 1907 and the ensuing financial crisis (Bensel 1991).

As banks collapsed and businesses failed, J. P. Morgan and his fellow wealthy investors poured millions into the banking system to provide the necessary liquidity to keep the crisis from destroying the economy. This bold move, coupled with the severity of the crisis, prompted Congress to take action (Bruner and Carr 2009). The 1907 national meltdown demonstrated the need for a new system, and Senate Majority Leader Nelson Aldrich realized it. With plans in mind for a system based in government-issued bonds, Aldrich formed and led a bipartisan commission to study the American monetary system and European central banking.

Aldrich's research would transform him. What he learned about the Bank of England, the German Bundesbank, and other European central banks helped him form a compelling vision. Abandoning his original schemes, Aldrich began sketching the beginnings of an American central bank (Law Librarians Society of Washington, DC 2014).

His blueprint was ambitious. With 15 branches strategically distributed throughout the United States, and united by a central bank headquartered in the District of Columbia, the new system would help manage a uniform elastic currency based on a combination of gold and commercial paper. Ideally, Aldrich wanted a central banking system independent of the government. But, understanding the political impracticality of a central bank unrestrained by public input, he incorporated a modicum of government oversight into his design and sought to convince others that decentralization would prevent corruption or undue political or banker influence.

While admirably constructed, Aldrich's design did not satisfy his critics. His detractors, chiefly Southern Democrats and Populist factions, feared Aldrich was swayed by his close ties to the banking industry. In stark contrast to Aldrich's plans, progressive Democrats favored a system owned and operated by the government. If the central bank was public property, Progressives envisioned it could be used to loosen Wall Street's current stranglehold on the American currency supply.

As Democrats grabbed control of Washington after the 1912 election, hope for passage of Aldrich's plan evaporated—but its influence had taken root. In a Democrat-backed bill proposed by Oklahoma's Robert Owen, a new system was proposed that would diverge from Aldrich's vision in only one significant way: it placed control over selecting its powerful board of directors with the government. Riding a wave of partisan support through Congress, Owen's bill passed in late 1913 to become the Federal Reserve Act, and the Fed was born.

* * *

To begin building this new system, the Reserve Bank Operating Committee (RBOC) was commissioned by Congress to select the locations for the regional banks. The committee members—Treasury Secretary William McAdoo, Agriculture Secretary David Houston, and the incoming Comptroller of the Currency John Williams—were quick to tackle the monumental task. Surveying armies of bankers from thousands of banks and launching a "listening tour" of almost 20 cities linked by 10,000 miles, the committee eventually chose 12 locations from a list of 37 potential sites (Binder and Spindel 2013).

In examining RBOC archives, scholars Sarah Binder and Mark Spindel have identified the embedded political and financial strategies that might have guided the committee's choices. Their "political model" assumes that the committee's close ties to Democratic president Wilson influenced the committee's hand; their "financial model," as might be expected, assumes the committee's decisions were made for economic reasons (Binder and Spindel 2013). The evidence, however, immediately casts doubt on the latter model. Records of the committee's banker survey reveal that the financial community believed fewer locations would centralize finance and minimize coordination problems and many bankers consequently wanted only the minimum of eight regional banks required by the Federal Reserve Act. Equally trying for the financial model is the fact that, at the time, 5 of the 12 regional bank locations were outside the country's 12 largest financial hubs (see Figure 1.1 for details). Finance, it seems, took a backseat in the committee's choices.

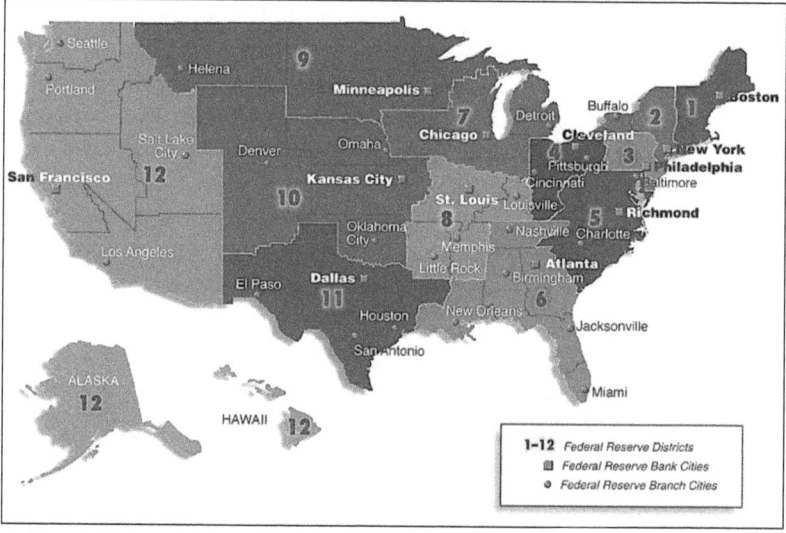

Figure 1.1 Twelve Federal Reserve district boundaries as they were drawn by the RBOC.

In contrast, the conspicuous clustering of the bank locations around Democratic and Progressive strongholds presented an obvious political advantage:

> The RBOC sought to make up for the deficit of credit in the South, and thus sought out southern locations when looking to extend the reserve system beyond the nation's financial centers in the East. In doing so, of course, the RBOC also placed a coveted financial resource in the heart of the Democratic South. (Binder and Spindel 2013, 10)

While the locations and the number of the regional banks ran counter to financial strategy, regional boundaries were equally suspect. As column two of Table 1.1 demonstrates, the population of each of the districts seems as irrelevant to the boundaries as finance was to the bank locations.

This is epitomized by the placement of a reserve bank in Kansas City. Despite being the country's 20th largest city and 18th largest banking center, Kansas City was selected as one of the final 12 over bigger financial hubs in more centralized locations (relative to other regional banks) like Denver, Omaha, and Lincoln. Why choose Kansas City? Here again, politics is the prime suspect. Unlike those other locations, Kansas City was home to a powerful Democratic political machine. The apparent motivations behind

Table 1.1 Federal Reserve district populations in 1913 and 2000

District	1913 Population (%)	2000 Population (%)
San Francisco	6	19
Atlanta	12	15
Chicago	17	13
Richmond	9	10
Dallas	5	8
Philadelphia	11	8
New York	10	7
Boston	7	5
Kansas City	6	4
St. Louis	8	4
Cleveland	5	4
Minnesota	4	3

Note: Estimates calculated by the Federal Reserve Bank of San Francisco. Data originally from the US Census Bureau (Federal Reserve Bank of San Francisco 2015).

the committee's decisions highlight an important theme in the history of the Fed: at/during nearly every step of the system's creation, politics was a driving force.

Those politics are still on display today—in the form of systematic over-representation. Using the 2000 census data, column three of Table 1.1 clearly exhibits the significant over-representation and influence that Minnesota, Cleveland, Kansas City, St. Louis, and Boston have in the modern Fed. Residents in the Minnesota Fed district are, for example, more than six times as represented as those in the San Francisco district. This issue is exacerbated by Fed voting policies: the president of the New York Fed has a permanent vote on the Federal Open Market Committee, whereas the other regional bank presidents rotate roughly every three years. In other words, residents of the NY Fed district are nearly 7.5 times more represented than those residing in the San Francisco district. In the early years of the Fed, when the Board also included the Treasury secretary and the Comptroller of Currency, this representation dynamic was even more complex (Flaherty 2010).

* * *

The passage of the Federal Reserve Act and the January 1914 creation of the branch banks led to massive changes in the banking system. The Act compelled all nationally chartered private banks to join the Federal Reserve System and accept the newly established national currency. These private banks were now required to purchase specified nontransferable stock in their regional Federal Reserve bank and to set aside a stipulated amount of non-interest-bearing reserves within their respective reserve bank. Instead of being forced, state chartered banks were invited to become members of the system, and many did because of its numerous benefits; in addition to borrowing privileges, members became a key constituency for American banking's new establishment.

Members of Congress might have been this establishment's formal principals, but, until Depression-era reforms were instituted, regional interests drove Fed policy. Regional directors and staff were selected by the local business community to represent local business interests. An impotent board of directors combined with economic diversity of the regions left the regional banks free to set their own rates.

Within this independence, however, was the seed of centralization. It didn't take long for investors to notice, and take advantage of, the arbitrage opportunities created by the disparity between reserve bank rates. Regional banks were forced to act and decided to unite behind a singular policy. Instead of setting their own rates, the regional banks began to follow the lead of the Federal Reserve Bank of New York—the highest volume exchange bank. Without government interference, the Federal Reserve was slowly silencing dissent and quietly beginning its march toward centralization.

By the time the roaring twenties slowed in 1927, the New York Fed was the de facto capital of the entire system, and its governor, Benjamin Strong, sat on the throne. No central bank in American history had survived more than 20 years, and Strong was undoubtedly concerned with upholding the legitimacy of the young system. Unfortunately, Strong's reaction to the 1927 recession would become a lightning rod for criticism of the Fed and helped lead the United States into disaster. Perhaps failing to see the recession as a natural market correction or perhaps pandering to Wall Street banking interests, Strong decided to lower interest rates to sustain rapid growth, and the entire system followed suit (Moss and Bolton 2009). The economy overheated, finally collapsing in the stock market crash of 1929. Strong would never live to see it. Dying shortly after the 1927 slowdown, Strong became an easy, defenseless scapegoat for Fed officials looking to point fingers.

Regardless of where the blame lay, the Fed still had chaos on its plate—and the turmoil only escalated. In 1930, with the stock market still reeling, the enormous, privately owned, but authoritatively titled Bank of United States failed, and the Fed, still under fire for 1927, had to decide whether or not to step in (Moss and Bolton 2009). It was a perilous decision. The Bank of United States was massive, and its demise would throw gasoline on an economy already in flames. But, if the Fed did step in, it could encourage the Bank of United States, and other banks, to play fast and loose—confident that even if they took the plunge the central bank would dive in after them. But there were more layers yet. While Wall Street, terrified of another downturn, was begging for intervention, the Fed was also invested in appeasing Capitol Hill, and the Fed's democratically elected Congressional principals sought to distance themselves from the bankers who had lost their constituents' hard-earned money. Pinned between private and public interests, the Fed let the bank capsize.

The Fed's challenges did not end there: the question of rescuing one bank quickly led to a larger question about the entire basis for our monetary structure. By the end of 1931 much of Europe, including the United States' largest trade partner, Britain, had gone off the gold standard. The Fed, bound to gold by law, needed an act of Congress to abandon it. The Fed never asked. Instead, following New York's lead, the Fed elected to pump liquidity into the system in the most cautious way possible: lend out at high rates and only on good collateral. In response, Congress criticized this meek policy and suggested a bolder move by the Fed: loaning on all collateral. To the Fed, this proposal was more of a populist push than shrewd policy, and in a show of budding independence, it stood its ground.

The central bank's decision to stay on gold arguably not only made the Depression much more severe in the early 1930s, but also made the recovery equally robust. The decades to come saw a renewed faith in the US dollar, and that faith was backed by gold.

* * *

The Fed began its journey toward centralization without a formal legal mandate. The leadership of the New York Fed throughout the 1920s and into the 1930s accelerated that evolution and pushed the Fed away from Congressional appeals and toward economic data analysis and technocratic policy. It would take several more decades for this progression to come to fruition, but the steps taken in the Fed's first 20 years laid the essential groundwork. The Fed was about to enter a period of protracted conflict with the Treasury, whose power and influence weighed heavily on the central bank throughout its youth. But conflict led to progress. The middle of the twentieth century would witness the birth of a powerful new central bank: centralized, independent, and technocratic.

2

Independence: Wars, Depression, and Politics

The executive branch dominated the Fed through the 1940 and early 1950s. Although Congress held sway over the board of directors and the Fed's relative independence mitigated the White House's supremacy, the executive branch's inevitable control sprung from the institutional design of the Fed—and the power of a unitary executive. The Treasury provided the muscle behind this control, and decades of conflict between Fed officials and Treasury officials provided the political fires that forged the development of today's independent and transparent reserve system. This chapter continues the account of the political battles, financial reforms, and world wars that fostered the Fed through the Great Depression to their independence and beyond.

* * *

In the face of 25 percent unemployment and a collapsing financial sector, Franklin Roosevelt instituted his New Deal when he took office in 1933. Through increased government spending and institutional reforms, the New Deal sought to stimulate demand and provide support for the impoverished. But, like any deal, Roosevelt's came with price—especially for the Fed. Weakened by the steep recession and its apparent inaction during the crisis, the Fed could only watch as the New Deal measures came into effect—measures that meant structural changes to the central banking system.

The New Deal unleashed a tidal wave of fiscal expenditure, reform, and regulation, including today's now-familiar regulatory organizations. Born out of the Glass-Steagall Act, the Federal Deposit Insurance Coporation (FDIC) was created to insure private bank deposits. The Securities Act of 1933 comprehensively regulated the securities industry, and the Securities Exchange Act of 1934 created the Securities and Exchange Commission (SEC). The SEC alleviated some pressure on the Fed to regulate financial markets and the FDIC secured individual deposits and provided a clear mandate that the Fed was to be a systemic lender of last resort.

Glass-Steagall had a dramatic effect on the Fed as a regulator, but it was not until 1935 that the monetary side of the Fed faced genuine reforms. These reforms renamed the board, dropped the Treasury secretary and Comptroller of Currency from it, and dictated that all Board nominees would be subject to presidential appointment and Senate confirmation. These reforms should have put the Fed in the hands of the Senate, but the executive branch would become the real guiding force behind US economic policy as America headed into the next global conflict.

* * *

Shortly after Japanese bombs laid waste to Pearl Harbor, Federal Reserve and Treasury officials convened to discuss how to finance the war. To back American military efforts, they decided to set rates for bonds at 2.5 percent and a range of 0.5–0.75 percent for bills. The Fed sought to utilize open market operations to maintain interest rate levels, but Treasury preferred a different method: manipulation of excess reserves. Traditionally, the Fed has controlled the monetary supply through the interest rate. The interest rate is, effectively, the price of money; the more expensive money is to borrow, then the less money is borrowed, and, consequently, the less money there is in the system. By the same process, cheaper money leads to an expansion in the monetary supply. The Treasury wanted the Fed to break with these traditional methods and control of the monetary supply by directly targeting a specific quantity. The Fed saw the Treasury's strategy as outside their Congressional mandate, but they were rapidly undercut by the Treasury's unilateral decision to peg interest rates at 0.375 percent for treasury bills, short term, and 2.5 percent for treasury bonds, long term (Wicker 1969). By pegging interest rates, the Treasury gave the Fed only one way of controlling the monetary supply—reserve manipulation. The pegged rates also forced the Fed into another paradox: the central bank had to choose between appearing unpatriotic and allowing government debt to go unsupported or continuing to buy and sell securities, despite their wishes, to maintain desired rates. With its back against the wall, the Fed acquiesced.

Treasury's policy, however, had unexpected consequences. By pegging rates, the Treasury effectively took away the fluidity of the government securities market. Because rates were fixed, bonds became safe as cash while also providing a return, and banks converted their assets to bonds. Banks used bonds, in other words, as excess reserves with interest. Since the banks avoided Treasury bills, the Federal Reserve was forced to buy up massive amounts to maintain the static interest rates and the money supply expanded rapidly (Board of Governors of the Federal Reserve System 1948).

Fed officials quickly realized that these policies were not sustainable from a price stability perspective, but it didn't matter. As long as the war continued, they had no choice but to continue the policy—effectively ceding control of the government securities market, and monetary policy in general, to the Treasury. Had the Fed pursued its independent policy, interest rates would have been flexible. Instead of only bonds, banks would have had an incentive to buy Treasury bills too, mitigating the severity of the ensuing inflation. But Treasury violated their initial agreement, and Fed officials failed to assert the central bank's independence. Once the Fed initially submitted to the Treasury, they could not have reversed course without being branded unpatriotic during wartime, which would likely have prompted Congress and President Truman to further cripple the Fed's already diminishing independence by inflicting even more reforms.

* * *

Even as World War II came to a close, the Treasury's low-rate policy remained. Forced to maintain the extremely low interest rates set at the beginning of the war, the Fed essentially granted control of the money supply to the Treasury. Despite meek objections from

Fed personnel, the Treasury continued to expand the total amount of monetary assets in the country with low bond and bill rates. The 1944 Bretton Woods Agreement would only make matters worse for the Fed. By establishing a system of fixed but adjustable exchange rates based on a 35 dollars per ounce gold price, the agreement left the Fed with less direct control over the cost of money, making their power over monetary policy all the more tenuous (Meltzer 2003). In the emerging postwar world, the Fed remained subordinate to the Treasury.

With World War II finally over, Congress began to stand up for the Fed in 1946. Containing an early version of the dual mandate, the Fed's famous charge to bolster employment and price stability, The Employment Act, granted the central bank the authority to direct policy to achieve "maximum employment and purchasing power" (Meltzer 2003). The Act indicated that the Fed had a different charge than the Treasury—and should behave accordingly. It also signaled that Congress would side with the Fed as Treasury's arguments for postwar fixed interest rates lost their luster.

* * *

Even as inflationary pressure built and a recession loomed, a stubborn Treasury continued to wave the same banner. While insisting that low interest rates were necessary to both maintain confidence in government credit and hold down the cost of postwar government debt, Treasury officials even went so far as to claim that controlling the money supply was not necessarily an effective means of reducing inflation. The Federal Reserve, however, "did not expect to maintain the wartime rate structure after the war," and tensions mounted (Meltzer 2010).

Throughout the Fed's postwar battle with the Truman Treasury, the Republican-controlled Congress was seen as sympathetic to the Fed's cause, and the clash between Capitol Hill and the Democratic White House provided just enough cover for the central bank to allow the bill rate to rise in 1947—earning them significant interest income. Due to the agreement that allowed them to raise the bill rate, the Fed turned over 90 percent of the revenue it generated back to the Treasury. This set a precedent, and the Fed has continued to turn over income to the Treasury ever since. In 2014, for example, the Fed gave the Treasury almost 100 billion (Board of Governors of the Federal Reserve System 2015b).

The end of bill targeting was another step toward independence, but the Fed remained bound by the Treasury's target rate for long-term bonds. When the pegged bill rate was lifted, the market was so far out of equilibrium that public purchase of Federal Reserve debt shifted from long-term securities to short-term securities. Thus, the Fed's decreased responsibility for the short-term market led to an increase in the long-term market. Despite greater involvement in bonds, the Fed took advantage of the increased demand in short-term securities. Unloading 1 billion dollars off their balance sheet, the Fed reduced financial ties with Treasury, but "political concerns continued to limit the Federal Reserve's ability to respond to postwar inflation" (Meltzer 2010).

* * *

Even 1946's spring budget surplus didn't faze a Treasury bent on maintaining wartime interest rates in a postwar world—a policy that stoked fears of inflation. Fed Chairman Marriner Eccles protested that the Treasury had turned the Fed into an "engine of inflation"; not coincidently, he would fail to be reappointed by Truman in 1948. Noted Fed historian and Carnegie Mellon economist Allan Meltzer (2010) notes, "The Federal Reserve shared the widespread concern among economists that the presence of a large, outstanding public debt limited the role of monetary policy." Fear that increasing interest rates could lead to deflation, a fear shared by President Truman, balanced this concern. Given the White House's worries about deflation, Chairman Eccles knew the political climate was not right for such a policy. Instead, to combat inflation, Congress passed a bill that increased reserve requirements. Forcing the Fed to pursue contractionary monetary policy that only served as catalyst to the recession, the bill backfired, crippling the economy.

The sudden economic downturn allowed the Fed to strike a deal with Treasury. Crafted in the summer of 1948, the deal empowered the Federal Open Market Committee (FOMC) to direct open market operations "[...] with primary regard to the general business and credit situation" (Board of Governors of the Federal Reserve System 1949). Since unemployment rose between 1948 and 1949 and prices slightly declined, the Fed-Treasury agreement permitted the Fed to lower interest rates in an attempt to stimulate the economy. This easing measure did not assert Fed control over monetary policy as Fed officials had hoped, and it remained unclear whether the Fed would have the flexibility to raise interest rates if the problem became one of inflation (Meltzer 2003).

In this lengthy struggle between the Fed (Board of Governors of the Federal Reserve System 2015c) and the Treasury (Board of Governors of the Federal Reserve System 2015a), Congress again came to the Fed's rescue. In 1949, newly elected Democratic Senator Paul Douglas held a series of hearings about interest rate policy. A career academic economist, Douglas's sympathies visibly sat with the central bank. Finding natural allies in the opposing party, Douglas was able to forge a strong, bipartisan interest in Fed autonomy. The Douglas hearings examined the extent to which the Fed's efforts at price stability were weakened by the Treasury's demands. The report stated:

> Do Federal Reserve officials determine the general level of interest rates, including yields on Governments, that they will establish so that the Treasury in fixing rates on new issues must conform to the decisions of the Federal Reserve? Or do Federal Reserve officials conform their general credit policies, including their support levels for Governments, to the pattern desired by the Treasury? The evidence presented to the subcommittee indicates that there is no simple answer to these questions. Federal Reserve and Treasury officials and staff members are in frequent consultation, and many decisions are agreed upon by the two agencies without marked differences of opinion. On some occasions when there were originally differences of opinion the Treasury has "gone along" with Federal Reserve requests for higher interest rates. But the evidence indicates that in a majority of the cases where the judgments of the two agencies differed it was the judgment of the Treasury that prevailed; the Federal Reserve was not willing to assert its independence and force market yields to rise above the yields that the Treasury wished to set on its new issues, thereby embarrassing the Treasury. It appears that in the absence of strong Treasury influence the Federal Reserve would have initiated a tighter monetary policy somewhat earlier and that this policy would have been carried further. (Joint Committee on the Economic Report 1950, 28–29)

In essence, the hearing report indicates that pressure from the Treasury had loosened the Fed's monetary policy. Continuing to back the central bank, the report also affirmed that "the primary power and responsibility, and cost of credit in general shall be vested in the duly constituted authorities of the Federal Reserve System" (Meltzer 2003). Concluding that controlling inflation trumped controlling federal debt, the report supported granting the Federal Reserve the freedom to raise interest rates.

Senator Douglas had demonstrated that leaders in Congress wanted an end to fixed interest rates and, perhaps more importantly, an independent Fed (Meltzer 2010). Solidifying their opposition to Congress and the Fed, the White House and Treasury disagreed—and ignored the report.

* * *

While the Fed may have gained a strong ally on Capitol Hill, conflict began growing inside its doors. At the start of 1950, a recession had some market actors—Wall Street in particular—rethinking old positions about Fed independence. Seeing the greater profit margins higher interest rates allowed for, Wall Street began pressuring government officials inside and outside the Fed to respond more directly to market conditions (Flaherty 2010). But inside the Fed this pressure from the banking community highlighted a growing division between former chairman—and current Board member—Marriner Eccles and Alan Sproul, president of the New York Fed.

Eccles and Sproul both fought for an independent central bank; they just wanted different principals. "Eccles saw the Federal Reserve as mainly a government agency regulating the financial industry and carrying out government policy," while Sproul "saw the Federal Reserve as mainly a financial institution, blending public and private control" (Meltzer 2003). These views mirrored the split between political and private control that had plagued the Fed since the Aldrich Plan.

While the Korean War put the Fed's internal debate on hold, it set the stage for yet another standoff between the central bank and the Treasury. Wartime spending once again ignited fears of inflation, forcing the FOMC to take action. Instead of raising interest rates themselves, the Fed requested that Treasury Secretary Snyder make 2.5 percent bonds ineligible for bank purchase to raise the short-term rate. Snyder refused. The Fed countered, increasing the discount rate. In response, Snyder announced a bond sale at 1.75 percent, conflicting with the new Fed rate. The bond sale was a failure, but the Treasury still refused to issue a 2.5 percent bond. Beginning a credit restraint policy, Fed officials continuously warned of rising inflationary pressure. Their efforts, however, were doomed by a Board "not willing to insist on an independent policy." "Politics," as Meltzer (2010) perfectly sums it up, "overrode anti-inflation policy."

Conflict between the Fed and Treasury continued through the fall of 1950—with doublespeak and lies coming from meetings at the highest level. At the conclusion of a meeting between Truman, Snyder, and Fed Chairman McCabe, Snyder gave a speech declaring that a 2.5 percent rate ceiling would remain. Snyder's declaration—violating the policy McCabe had agreed to—infuriated Fed officials, but more lies would follow.

* * *

The rising tensions between the Fed and Treasury didn't prevent the entire FOMC from meeting with President Truman in early 1951. In a statement released after the meeting, the White House reported, "The Federal Reserve Board has pledged its support to President Truman to maintain the stability of Government securities as long as the emergency lasts" (Eccles 1951). In a corresponding statement, the Treasury backed the White House, announcing that interest rate levels would be maintained for the duration of the Korean War. Both were false. The FOMC had never agreed to maintain the rate. In fact, Truman had never even asked (Eccles 1951).

But the Executive branch's deceit would backfire, providing the central bank with new allies in the press and giving additional momentum to its push for independence. On the heels of the deception, former Fed chairman Eccles released his personal notes from the meeting to the press. The *Sunday New York Times* and *Washington Post* boldly printed that Truman and Snyder had lied. Fed Chairman McCabe, in an attempt to reign in the growing conflict, sent timid letters to both Truman (McCabe 1951a) and Snyder (McCabe 1951b). But, before they could publicly respond, the financial community spoke out. In a speech at a Pennsylvania Bankers Association meeting, Aubrey Lanston—former assistant to the secretary of the Treasury—had strong words for the future of the Fed: "We believe it is most desirable that the Federal Reserve become more free than it has been in the past decade to follow a restrictive credit policy at times when this is needed" (Lanston 1951). A few weeks later, the Economists National Committee on Monetary Policy issued a press release titled "51 Members Urge the Importance of Restoring and Maintaining the Independence of the Federal Reserve System" (Economists' National Committee On Monetary Policy 1951). With bankers and economists rallying in support for the Fed, and the Administration's deceit exposed, it was clear that change was in the air and the financial press knew it, backing the Fed from that point forward.

Presidential lies weren't the only bombshell. Just as the Fed's camp began to swell with newfound support, the announcement was made that consumer prices rose at a 14 percent annual rate. Alarmed, Secretary of Defense James Forrestal became concerned about inflation and the rising costs of the Korean War. With Senator Douglas and his colleagues pushing for an independent Fed on Capitol Hill, Forrestal's valid concerns joined the chorus of voices calling for a Fed free of Treasury control.

Negotiations between the Fed and Treasury began almost immediately—culminating in the now-famous 1951 Fed-Treasury Accord. The Fed "agreed to share responsibility for the orderly marketing of government debt" and to buy 200 million dollars in 2.5 percent bonds at the next refunding. Additionally, the Fed would wait for Treasury approval before changing the discount rates over the next year. In return, Treasury let short-term rates rise and longer-term debt rise above the 2.5 percent rate. The publicly released agreement stated:

> The Treasury and the Federal Reserve System have reached full accord with respect to debt management and monetary policies to be pursued in furthering their common purpose to assure the successful financing of the Government's requirements and, at the same time, to minimize monetization of the public debt. (United States Treasury and Federal Reserve Board of Governors 1951)

Although it is considered by many to be the origin of Fed independence, the 1951 Accord was actually a meekly worded gentlemen's agreement. It was not official legislation or a binding contract. It did not change the legal status of the Fed or reform its organizational structure. While ending pegged interest rates, the Accord made no mention of optimal policy or long-term goals and, most importantly, it did not grant the Fed complete independence. As Douglas remarked shortly after the Accord, "It is not clear just what this agreement means." Although it does not actually mark the birth of central bank autonomy, the Accord served as a catalyst that led to the Fed's ultimate assertion of independence and strength.

* * *

Shortly after the Accord was signed, McCabe resigned as Chairman, and Truman selected William McChesney Martin to replace him. A Treasury Undersecretary and the top Accord negotiator for the Treasury, Martin had the pedigree to bridge the gap between the warring houses. The Treasury could breathe easy, convinced the central bank was in familiar hands; Fed officials, on the other hand, could trust the new chairman's lineage: Martin's father was the long-time president of the Federal Reserve Bank of St. Louis. As a former head of the New York Stock Exchange, Martin was a seasoned player with the skills to calm financial markets. Martin also understood that he was inheriting an institution "that had not pursued an independent policy since 1933" (Meltzer 2003). With the right mix of pedigree and politics, Martin was poised to be a powerhouse at the helm of the nation's banking system.

Truman, however, got a little more than he bargained for with his dream selection. Although the Accord had reduced Treasury's influence, the Fed was still bound to back a handful of Treasury efforts. In practice, this meant the "even keel" policy: the Fed held interest rates constant for two weeks before and after the sale of Treasury notes and bonds. Although it functionally limited the Fed, Martin was expected to maintain this type of coordination. However, Truman didn't know Martin as well as he thought. The new Fed chairman believed in "independence within the Government," and this, apparently, was more independence than Truman expected—or wanted—from Bill Martin. Disenchanted, the president would later refer to Martin as a "traitor" (Bremner 2004).

Given Truman's disappointment with the level of independence Martin sought for the Fed, it is clear that the president did not expect the Accord to actually unshackle the Fed from the Treasury—and neither did the Treasury. The Accord, it seems, was designed to placate the financial press, appease a few senators, and allow the administration to continue steamrolling the Fed.

* * *

It is interesting to note that despite Truman's anger toward Martin, the evidence doesn't actually support his ire. Fed policy in 1951 and 1952 was not the product of an independence-obsessed chairman. Martin's Annual Report of the Board of Governors of the Federal Reserve System for the year of 1952 states:

> The Federal Reserve System followed a policy of restraining the pace of credit expansion by making it necessary for member banks to borrow in order to obtain reserves. This put them under pressure to restrict expansion of their loans and investments. Thus discount operations at the Reserve Banks again became an effective instrument of credit policy, a further realization of the purposes envisaged by the Treasury-Federal Reserve accord of March 1951. (Martin 1953, 1)

The data, however, does not support the claim that the Fed tightened credit in 1951. In fact, the president's own economic report in 1953 indicates that the discount rate remained at 1.75 percent for all of 1951 and 1952 (Council of Economic Advisers 1953). The same report indicates that the Fed expanded both bank credit and the money supply through 1951 and 1952:

> In both 1951 and 1952, an expansion of Federal Reserve Bank credit was one of the factors which supplied commercial banks with reserves. During 1952, borrowing by member banks provided the greater amount of reserves from this source, while in the previous year the net increase in Federal Reserve Bank holdings of U. S. Government securities was more important. The average of Federal Reserve discounts in 1952 was more than one and one-half times greater than in 1951, but Federal Reserve holdings of Government obligations averaged about the same. The privately held money supply (including the bank deposits of State and local governments) expanded almost 9 billion dollars or about 5 percent in 1952, nearly as much as in the previous year. (Council of Economic Advisers 1953)

In contrast to some accounts, Martin did not immediately assert Fed independence or use the Accord as his shield during 1951 and 1952 (Meltzer 2010). In other words, Truman's traitor was not the turncoat he was made out to be.

* * *

Deserved or not, Truman's growing animosity toward Martin reflected the attitude virtually the entire Democratic Party, aside from Senator Douglas, had toward the Fed—an attitude not shared by the Republican Party. As the 1952 elections approached, the Republican Party platform formally backed Fed independence. They wanted a "Federal Reserve System [...] without pressure for political purposes from the Treasury or the White House" (Wilson 1992). Although important to warring factions in the government, the battle over central bank independence was not the conflict on most Americans' minds at the time. Tired of the bloody struggle in Korea—already in its third year—the nation clamored for peace. Leveraging this discontent, Republican Dwight Eisenhower swept the 1952 Presidential election, carrying 39 states.

Eisenhower immediately began work on foreign and domestic battlegrounds. In an effort to accelerate peace talks in Korea, Eisenhower made peace—or nuclear war—the only options. Ike's atomic power play worked, and the war came to a close in July of 1953. In the battle over the Fed, Eisenhower chose a more diplomatic route, strategically appointing George Humphrey as Treasury secretary and W. Randolph Burgess as assistant to the secretary. Humphrey believed that the Fed should handle the market for government securities (Wells 2004) and Burgess was a former Fed official. With Fed supporters in key positions at the Treasury, the stage was set for Martin to "restructure the relationship between the Fed and the Treasury" (Bremner 2004).

Noting the Accord's important role in the long road toward Fed independence, a 1953 report by Secretary Humphrey relates the history of the war between the Fed and the Treasury:

> In the years preceding the March 1951 accord, the Federal Reserve System, under Treasury domination, contributed substantially to inflation by artificial manipulation of the value of Government securities. During and after

World War II, the Federal Reserve System lost much of its independence. It was used by the Treasury to raise unprecedented amounts of money, and during the war this requirement completely overshadowed monetary policy. As long as the war was on and Government controls kept wages and prices pretty well in line, there wasn't so much trouble: But when in 1946 direct controls were removed without also concurrently releasing the Federal Reserve, the excesses of the war years brought inflation and hardship to millions of Americans. In the years from 1946 to 1951, the Federal Reserve was a prisoner of the Treasury policy in handling the national debt. Instead of allowing the natural increases in interest rates, the Federal Reserve focused major attention on making sure that the Treasury could handle the debt at low rates. This was not in the best interests of the country as a whole. It resulted in the absence of effective monetary policy until the accord of March 1951. As you gentlemen well know, the March 1951 accord partly restored effective monetary policy to its rightful place in our economy. It laid the groundwork for the policy which the present administration is pledged to continue. (US Treasury Department 1954, 248)

This same report also declared that the Eisenhower administration "assured the Federal Reserve System that it will have the prime responsibility for maintaining the money and credit situation free of artificial restraints in the best interests of all Americans" (US Treasury Department 1954). These words were not hollow. In 1952, the Joint Economic Committee report on Monetary Policy and Management of the Public Debt referenced the need for Fed Independence 56 times in just 80 pages (Joint Committee on the Economic Report 1952). By 1954, a comparable report from the Joint Economic Committee referenced the need for Fed independence just four times in 331 pages (Joint Committee on the Economic Report 1954).

After years of embittered conflict, the Fed had finally broken free, and the inauguration of Dwight Eisenhower was a defining moment in that struggle. With rates allowed to rise and inflation kept in check, the Fed's independence helped lead America into the most prosperous decade in its history.

* * *

The vast majority of scholarly literature treats the 1951 Accord as the Federal Reserve's independence day, but, as this chapter points out, there is much more to the story. The Accord was only one link in the long chain of political events that led to a liberated Fed. By acknowledging that Fed independence was achieved as a result of a series of political moves, rather than a legal contract or accord, this narrative highlights the ever-present role of politics in Fed policy. "Politics," as Alan Meltzer (2010) says, "was a dominant influence on Federal Reserve policy," and it remains so to this day.

Ultimately, the real question isn't where to date the birth of an independent central bank. Rather, the real question is how that independence changes policy—and how that policy influences markets. The survivor of a decades-long struggle over sovereignty, the Fed learned the value of autonomy—an autonomy it would later maintain through a policy of transparency.

3

Centralization: The Rise of Technocracy

Entering the 1950s with new leadership and newfound autonomy, the Federal Reserve was ripe for modernization. Spanning the next two decades, this chapter tells the story of the beginning of that change. Central to this narrative is the newly appointed chairman of the Fed, William Martin, and the role his influence and leadership would have in the Fed's transformation. During Martin's tenure, the slow push toward centralization that had begun during the Fed's infancy would accelerate, and the technological revolution outside its doors would be mirrored in the technocratic revolution unfolding within them.

While Fed transparency is addressed in the next few chapters—and is essential to the book as whole—it is important to note that the institution began embracing transparency as a direct result of the pivotal developments during this period. As educated, technically inclined policymakers joined the Fed's ranks during the 1950s and 1960s, the increasingly centralized, powerful, and technocratic institution appeared all the more intimidating and opaque to the public—and to its bureaucratic principals. President Nixon's comments after the 1960 presidential election serve as a perfect example of central bank ascendancy: the presidential candidate believed the central bank and its chairman to be so powerful that he blamed Martin's tight monetary policy for the Republican loss (Axilrod 2011a).

* * *

Although Martin lacked formal economic training, his background as head of the Import-Export Bank and the New York Stock

Exchange gave him a wealth of practical knowledge about the economy and a firm belief that economics was becoming an increasingly technical discipline. According to former Fed Staff Director Stephen Axilrod, Martin believed the Fed needed to keep pace with economic theory and practice to maintain credibility and establish good policy. Strong as Martin's convictions were, the old guard was slow to embrace new methods.

But there were changes. Regional banks began hiring young, academically trained economists, and, by the late 1950s, punch card computers were beginning to be used to conduct regression analysis on economic data (Axilrod 2011b). "Working at the Board: 1930s–1970s," a collection of writings by retired Fed officers, chronicles these changes, highlighting the role played by computing:

> A major change that developed over several decades has been in the way data and other information are assembled, worked on, stored, and updated. For a large part of the Board's history, these tasks were handled with what today many would consider very primitive tools: the desk calculator that was used for all data manipulation and ground out the results of simple operations; the manual typewriter that provided final copy only after uncounted retypings of successive drafts; the fourteen-column card that preserved statistical data (entered and updated by hand) and was stored in a clerk's private file case; the nonstatistical records usually kept on pieces of paper in someone's desk drawer....] Nevertheless, a relatively large force of statistical clerks and other record keepers turned out a lot of work with these tools, though it did not need to be, and was not, the complex and sophisticated output demanded in recent years. With the gradual shift through semiautomatic equipment to higher and higher levels of technology, employee skills have needed to be upgraded as well, and employment qualifications have risen. (Stockwell 1989, 2)

The usage of new data storage, aggregation, and analysis techniques required a more sophisticated staff, reinforcing the need for what Martin had already seen. The movement to improve the Fed was gaining steam, but critics of the central bank remained dissatisfied.

To learn from their critiques, Martin requested that Board staffer James Knipe gather, document, and explain these criticisms in a report from early February of 1962. The criticisms Knipe recorded from the Congressional Joint Economic Committee between 1959 and 1961 include:

1. Monetary policy is not very effective in three areas.
2. Monetary policy is too effective in three other areas.
3. The Federal Reserve System is not efficiently integrated into the administration.
4. The Federal Reserve System is not organized to function efficiently.
5. Federal Reserve operational results are handicapped by slippages, time lags, inadequacies and ambiguities.
6. The Federal Reserve is unduly, and wrongly, influenced by private banking interests.
7. The Federal Reserve promotes high interest rates to make more profits for lenders.
8. The Federal Reserve shortens economic upswings and stunts national economic growth. (Knipe 1962)

In his report, Knipe responds by pointing to the impossible choices faced by the Fed:

The institutional structure of the American economy in 1961 is one in which, as a result of the increased strength of highly-organized power blocs—labor, industry, agriculture—prices will have a tendency to rise whenever men and machines are operating at anywhere near to capacity. The purchasing power of the dollar is, therefore, subject to possible further deterioration within the next few years. As an important agency especially interested in the integrity of the dollar, the Federal Reserve will find itself again in the unenviable position of having to decide whether or not to restrain what it looks on as "inflationary excesses," at times when its critics may regard the economy's performance as unsatisfactory, and not even near to "inflationary excesses." (Knipe 1962, 68)

In essence, what critics may perceive as a central bank that "stunts national economic growth" is actually a central bank committed to its primary charge: "the integrity of the dollar." Pinned between the criticism it would face if it allowed for excess inflation and the criticism it would face if it "shorted economic upswings," the Fed was, as Knipe puts it, in an "unenviable position" (Knipe 1962).

*   *   *

Regardless of equity, the institution would continue to receive targeted criticism from Congress. Beginning in the 1950s and continuing into the 1970s, two of the most ardent Fed critics were Democratic Congressman Wright Patman (Texas) and Senator William Proxmire (Wisconsin). Leading their respective chambers' banking committees and many relevant subcommittees, Patman and Proxmire held tremendous sway: "When the Fed wanted a change in banking legislation, it was usually through these two chairmen that it had to proceed" (Stockwell 1989). Described by some former Fed officers an "inquisition," their oversight meant a nightmarish preparation process by central bank representatives:

> Patman was a populist, who regarded the Fed's occasional tight money forays as an oppression of the common man. Proxmire was a thrifty liberal, who advocated activist government but detested spendthrift bureaucrats and inefficient programs. Each of them found plenty of opportunities to try to trim the Fed's wings. A hearing before either of these gentlemen was something of an ordeal. Word of a new invitation to testify before either one was typically greeted around the Board with the institutional equivalent of a sigh. Preparations for the appearance were strenuous. Often a very substantial support document was required. Weeks and sometimes months of staff time were spent in its preparation. The testimony itself often included a good deal of grilling of the Fed witness by the committee chairman, rather in the style of a determined prosecuting attorney. It was a rare day when the Fed's representative could return from such a session and say "I got what I wanted." (Stockwell 1989, 26)

Not only did preparation for their hearings require significant staff hours, they often resulted in voluntary Fed budget cuts to keep their critics satisfied:

> Sometimes Patman and Proxmire would turn the tables on the Board by introducing some proposed new legislation that would take away some cherished Fed power or privilege. Bringing budgets of the Board or the Federal Reserve Banks under congressional control was a favorite thrust, and one the Fed regularly resisted. To the Fed, this breached the carefully crafted insulation from pressure politics that had been a key part of the legislation that had created it. As a practical matter, the Fed was a "cash cow" for the federal government, (a byproduct of its congressionally given power to create money) rather than a net user of federal budgetary

resources, and every Federal Reserve spokesman knew that. To help prove groundless the recurrent charge by Patman and Proxmire that the Fed was a wasteful spender of resources, the Board often turned the budget screws as tight on itself and the Federal Reserve Banks as the Administration and the Congress were endeavoring to do to the rest of the federal government. Nobody on the Board staff enjoyed these episodes. In fact, the Board was not a lavish spender to begin with, so often what resulted were marginal spending curtailments that took nicks out of a sizable number of cherished projects, programs, and perquisites, of which the most important were undoubtedly staff salary increases. (Stockwell 1989, 27)

These cuts notably sliced into staff salaries, limiting the rate at which the Fed was able to grow and acquire technically proficient staff.

But the Fed would not let financial belt-tightening completely cripple its progress. In 1963, Daniel Brill, director of Research and Statistics at the Board, convinced Martin that the Fed needed more "expert economists" (Axilrod 2011b), and, as a result, the Fed hired a series of highly trained economists from top-tier doctoral programs to work in Brill's division. By the mid-1960s, the International Finance division headed by Robert Solomon had also begun hiring technically inclined PhD economists, and, of the five documented finalists for an appointment to the Federal Reserve Board in 1964, four had advanced degrees: three PhDs and a JD (Dillon 1964). By comparison, at that time only about 40 percent of Americans had completed high school and only about 10 percent of adults were college educated. As the technical skills and training of the Fed's staff increased, the education gap between the central bank and public it served only widened, and a new, technocratic entity was taking shape.

* * *

The shift that took place during the second half of the twentieth century was dramatic. During the entire 40-year period between 1914 and 1954, the whole Federal Reserve System employed just 81 PhD economists and 14 MA, MBA, or JDs; there are an additional 44 people with unknown educational backgrounds. In 1931, the Federal Reserve Board employed just ten staff members. This number had grown to 22 by 1941 and 34 by 1951. Even five years into

William Martin's tenure as Fed chairman—1956—the Board still employed only 42 staff members. By contrast, in 2013 the Federal Reserve Board alone employs over 450 people; 296 of them are PhD economists (Board of Governors of the Federal Reserve System 2015c). That is, nearly four times as many PhD economists that the entire Federal Reserve System employed over the course of its first 40 years. And these figures do not count the massive staffing shift at regional banks.

Although staffing data from the regional banks is difficult to obtain because they are private entities not required to comply with the Freedom of Information Act, the available data also indicates that broad steps toward technocracy took place at regional Fed banks across the United States. Table 3.1 provides data on the background of regional bank presidents beginning in 1950. As this table illustrates, since the middle of the twentieth century the regional Fed banks have almost uniformly made strides toward being led by a president with either vast government experience as a public servant or a PhD.

The background of the regional bank presidents is particularly interesting because unlike the Board staff, who are selected by other staff for their analytical skills, the regional bank presidents are selected by the regional bank directors who represent the local business community in each region. This makes them the least likely to be selected based on academic qualifications and most likely to be selected based on business connections. Given that even these bank presidents have shifted toward being trained economists, it

Table 3.1 Regional Bank president backgrounds

Year	Banker/lawyer	Economist/public servant
1950	11	1
1960	8	4
1970	6	6
1979	5	7
1987	5	7
1995	3	9
2000	1	11
2010	2	10
2012	1	11

Note: This data was collected from each regional Fed bank's historical information.

is reasonable to assume that the directors of the regional banks deemed it necessary to have a technically trained bank president so that he might be able to understand the increasingly complex methods, models, and data presented by Board staff at Federal Open Market Committee (FOMC) meetings.

* * *

A pivotal period during this transition, the 1960s are best described by the staff who lived through them:

> The decade of the 1960s soon brought a fresh breeze to both the nation and the Federal Reserve. The election of 1960 put a young and vigorous President in the White House. He exuded confidence in rational thought. He arrived with some fresh ideas, and he was in the market for more. Accordingly, in a number of his early appointments he chose highly trained, intellectually curious individuals with forward-looking attitudes. They brought new ideas of their own and of other thinkers into policy circles. [...] In this atmosphere of intellectual challenge the Board staff responded vigorously. Friendly debates on policy issues great and small were common in the Board offices and over the cafeteria tables. The directors of the two research divisions, Arthur Marget and later Ralph Young for the Division of International Finance and Jack Noyes and later Dan Brill for the Division of Research and Statistics, were open to bringing in outside experts to exchange ideas. Brill was particularly adept at drawing thought-provoking scholars of varied backgrounds into the Board's offices for occasional talks or short stays. A somewhat more collegial tone came to pervade the halls of the Board. The Board even established a panel of outstanding academic consultants, who provided some very stimulating exchanges in their periodic meetings around the Board table. (Stockwell 1989, 21)

As this account attests, the era was characterized by its academic discourse, as Fed officials deliberately pursued the improvement of the central bank's intellectual environment. The Fed's relationship to the government, interestingly, is only referenced once in the passage, highlighting President Kennedy, but the narration focuses on the spirit of open inquiry he brought with him and the technocratic changes it helped inspire. This perspective on the Fed's relationship with the government points to the self-sufficiency the central bank saw itself as possessing. The executive branch, the Fed's former principal, is now pictured as a contributing partner. Times, it appears, had indeed changed.

* * *

During the 1960s, the Fed began a long tradition of authoring data-driven documentation. In 1964, the Fed rolled out the first edition of the "Green Book." These reports, formally entitled "Current Economic and Financial Conditions," are still distributed prior to each FOMC meeting and consist of a summary of the current economy, recent developments in the economy, and current financial conditions. A year later, the Board staff rolled out the first edition of the "Monetary Policy Recommendations"; like its counterpart, this too earned a moniker and became known as the "Blue Book" (Federal Open Market Committee 2012). Both the Green and Blue Books originated from the Board staff—not the regional banks—a fact that demonstrates the increased centralization of Fed policy in the mid-1960s. Given that each region is specifically charged with examining its own economic conditions, the Board's responsibility for analysis of national data undercut district bank personnel—leaving them without a technical data source to express opinions and preferences during FOMC meetings. Although subtle, the books were yet another sign of the future of the Fed as an increasingly centralized and information-oriented institution.

* * *

With a culture of healthy intellectual debate, sophisticated, highly trained personnel, and concrete mechanisms to convey research to key policymakers, the Fed would enter the next era armed. The central bank's own records echo this sentiment, affirming that by the end of the 1960s "the Board had equipped itself with a new generation of tools for economic analysis, a new managerial system, and a new generation of staff leadership with which to respond to the challenges of the 1970s" (Stockwell 1989).

4

Transparency: Data Meets Democracy

Like the 1950s and 1960s, the Fed's next era had its own defining leader: Paul Volker. Martin had shaped the Fed into a more centralized, powerful, and modern machine, and when Volker arrived on the scene—after two lackluster chairmen came and went—he would continue that tradition. Under his guidance, the Fed would continue its march from democracy to technocracy. This transformation would measurably increase the central bank's effectiveness, but it would also obscure its processes and the motivations behind its policy. As the previous chapter briefly mentioned, this opacity—this mixture of complex bureaucracy, complex processes, and complex data—made improving the lines of communication between the Fed and the government and the public an absolute necessity. What the Fed eventually grew to understand was the necessity of transparency, but that understanding would not be easily earned.

* * *

The 1970s began with the retirement of William Martin, the Fed's longest serving chairman. To replace Martin, President Nixon chose noted business cycle economist Arthur Burns, but his appointment, however, was not without complications. As the chair of the Council of Economic Advisers under President Nixon, he had built a rapport with the president, which led to the perception that Nixon would unduly influence policy. In addition, despite his business cycle expertise, Burns was also known to lack strong quantitative skills. These perceptions combined with uncontrolled inflation during his tenure meant that Burns's legacy was a lack of policy credibility, rather than any significant progress.

In large part, the lackluster achievements of the 1970s can be attributed to three factors:

1. The collapse of the post–World War II Bretton Woods system of international finance, which turned the US dollar into a fiat currency.
2. The political pressure placed on the Fed from the Nixon administration.
3. The new regulatory and transparency laws that increased the Fed's responsibilities.

Of the three, the collapse of Bretton Woods had the largest and most direct economic impact. As a result of the famous "Nixon Shock," the president's decision to unilaterally abandon the gold standard in August of 1971, many foreign countries chose to hold dollars as a reserve currency. This increased demand for dollars prompted White House officials to call Fed Board Director of Research and Statistics, Charles Partee, to the White House to emphasize that all policy decisions should help grow M2—the government's preferred measure of money supply (Axilrod 2011b). The dollar was in uncharted territory as both a fiat currency and a global reserve currency, and this new status—coupled with White House pressure—exacerbated inflation through the decade.

While Bretton Woods was certainly a powerful factor, many historical and political accounts of this era focus on the role of the Nixon/Burns dynamic in Fed policy, and the intricacies of this relationship were on full display in the period leading up to the 1972 election (Axilrod 2011a). At the time, Burns was not only the chairman of the Fed but the chair of the newly formed Committee on Interests and Dividends (CID) as well. Since the CID was designed to deal with wage and price controls, Burns's two roles conflicted: easing credit would make wage and price controls easier to implement, making his CID job easier, while at the same time jeopardizing the integrity of the dollar, the maintenance of which was his primary job as Fed chairman. Even if Nixon was not directly pressuring Burns, by appointing him to these dual roles he pressured the Fed chairman to adopt an easier monetary policy. In addition, despite post hoc Congressional criticism, Burns was encouraged to ease monetary policy through 1972 by members of Congress from both parties (Woolley 1986). Ultimately, the ineffective policy and perceived lack of political independence by the Fed Chairman contributed to rampant inflation—and the declining credibility of the central bank.

Stephen Axilrod, a former Fed staff director, offers one insider's perspective on the leadership of Arthur Burns:

> It was not that Burns... did not make a sustained effort to be a leader and to influence the policy decisions made by the FOMC. He most certainly did [...] But his actions were, as the now common expression has it, "inside the box." They were basically maneuvers, not grand performances that might have persuaded an audience (his fellow policymakers, for instance, not to mention the country as a whole) to see the economy and policy from a paradigmatically different viewpoint. (Axilrod 2011a, 64)

Unlike his predecessor, Burns maneuvered strictly within the existing confines of the institution, never testing its limits, expanding its scope, or exploring new ways to solve new or old problems.

Problematic leadership, however, did not seem to be the only major challenge facing the central bank at the time. An internal examination of the Fed highlights reveals a third major contributor to the Fed's underwhelming decade: the litany of new responsibilities the central bank took on. Their obligations, it seems, were endless:

> Massive data gathering, numbers crunching, and monitoring as the Fed did its part... to contain inflation by freezes, controls, voluntary restraints, and similar programs in 1971–74; adapting Board procedures and rules to the invasive Freedom of Information and Government in Sunshine legislation of 1974 and 1976; overhauling all the Board's regulations to make them more readable, to update them, to cut out deadwood, and to ease regulatory burdens; adapting to an increasingly demanding series of new reporting and recordkeeping requirements by the Congress; developing a national network of computerized regional centers for over-night check clearance; developing, together with other federal banking supervisors, uniform examination procedures; and initiating a long-term squeeze on banks and bank holding companies to improve capital ratios. (Stockwell 1989, 29)

Further examination of this era reveals the enormous workload of the Board staff in the 1970s:

> The Board held an average of 139 meetings yearly during the decade. The Governors were required to prepare for discussion of each agenda item, involving a heavy reading and study load. The Secretary's office had to prepare the Boardroom for meetings, prepare the agenda, and keep the official record [...] The Legal Division produced ninety-three proposed and final regulations, interpretations, and policy statements in 1970; 102 in 1977, and 159 in 1978: an average of 126 a year in the 1970s. The Board's legal submissions to the Federal Register took up 346 pages in 1970 and 899 pages in 1979. The division counts twenty-five major pieces of legislation passed in the 1970s affecting the Fed. [...] Production of news releases covering proposed and final regulations, policy statements, and like substantive subjects rose from fifty-one in 1970, to seventy-one in 1975 and to ninety-two in 1979... The Chairman and other Board members testified before the Congress seven times during 1970, an average of fifteen times a year in the first half of the decade and an average of forty-two times a year in the last five years, including sixty appearances in 1979. The Board established a Freedom of Information Office in 1974 under the amended FOI Act. The FOI office answered 3,969 queries under the act that year, 5,112 in 1979, and an average of 4,455 from 1974 to 1979, rejecting only 2.4 percent of requests received (under FOI Act exemptions). (Stockwell 1989, 30)

This account concludes with a telling statement: "While the Board's work grew manifold, its staff grew during the 1970s less than two-thirds, from 902 to 1,451" (Stockwell 1989, 30). These figures mark enormous bureaucratic growth, but considering the Congressional pressure limiting the expansion of the Fed's personnel, it actually highlights the tremendous growth of the Fed's responsibilities during this era.

While the scope of the duties was certainly daunting, it is also important to note the nature of what was required, specifically, the new transparency mandates that now filled the Fed's workload. Because of the central bank's inability to enact internal reform in the face of an inflationary crisis, the Fed had effectively surrendered its first mover advantage—its ability to reform itself before an outside authority could—to Congress. Impatient with tepid progress, Congress pressured the struggling central bank to move toward greater disclosure and greater transparency, and the Fed's efforts toward those ends increased dramatically. As the passage attests, the Fed testified to Congress in the second half of the decade almost three times as often as it did during the first half, and in 1979, it churned out nearly twice as many news releases about its activities as it did in 1970.

After these less formal attempts to compel the Fed toward more transparency, Congress ultimately passed the Federal Reserve Reform Act of 1977. The Act gave the legislature more control and oversight in the Fed. Whereas previously the President could freely appoint the chair and vice chair of the Board, Congress now mandated Senate approval for those positions and demanded quarterly reports as well. Perhaps most important from a policy perspective, the Fed Reform Act established the explicit goal of promoting maximum employment and price stability, making the dual mandate a statutory obligation from that point forward. Dictating that the Fed maximize growth, minimize inflation, and promote price stability, the 1978 Humphrey-Hawkins Act strengthened the dual mandate's influence on Fed policy (Flaherty 2010). While not revolutionary from a policy perspective, these pieces of legislation do demonstrate an essential historical lesson: if the central bank fails to reform itself, its autonomy will soon come under fire. In other words, the Fed's independence has been maintained by its ability to evolve.

* * *

These reforms wouldn't have the immediate impact Congress intended, as Burns's successor was an even less capable leader: William Miller. Formerly a successful CEO, Miller held the post for only 17 months, he then became Treasury secretary, and his brief tenure demonstrated to many that the skills required to effectively run the central bank were far different from those best suited to private enterprise. Unlike the top-down, vertical integration of major corporations, the Fed's structure bears far more resemblance to a wheel: a central authority uniting many smaller arms all working toward progress. Stephen Axilrod characterizes Miller's struggles with the chairmanship as follows:

> The whole monetary process involved a bureaucratic apparatus that was unfamiliar and in many ways trying. Depending on whether a decision was to be made by the board or by the FOMC, either six or eleven other

people beside the chairman had equal say in it. His colleagues' underlying motivations often were not clearly expressed, if expressed at all. Implementation of a decision relied on policy levers that—because of economic uncertainties, market complexities, unpredictable attitudinal shifts, and long lags—were not well or clearly linked to the institution's ultimate objectives. Even if long-term goals might be easily stated (it took no effort to favor price stability and growth, for example), how to approach them, what objectives should be emphasized in the nearer term, and how best to reconcile possible conflicts among them were always up for negotiation. (Axilrod 2011a, 77–78)

Under Miller's weak leadership, the Fed continued to cede its first mover advantage to Congress, who continued to pressure the Fed for increased disclosure.

* * *

After the ambivalence of the Burns's chairmanship and the ineffectual nature of Miller's, the Fed faced a crisis of confidence. The American public held diminished respect for the institution, and its inability to effectively combat inflation had fueled an increasingly severe political backlash, particularly from Congress. Then in 1979, President Carter appointed Paul Volcker, former Fed staffer, Treasury official, and sitting president of the Federal Reserve Bank of New York, to be Fed chairman. Volcker's tenure was marked by a technocratic shift that encouraged new methods in monetary policy, which helped rein in inflation and restore the central bank's standing. As a seasoned veteran of both the Fed and the Treasury, Volker had a vast amount of technical knowledge, a great sense of the bureaucratic barriers within the institution, and, unlike Miller, a deep understanding of the consensus-building nature of the chairman's position. Despite lacking a legal justification, Volcker would utilize innovative policy, bureaucratic maneuvering, and direct public communication to reshape the Federal Reserve (Axilrod 2011b).

* * *

Volker's capable leadership, however, wasn't the only ingredient to his reign's success. Despite new responsibilities, increased workload, and the lack of effective leadership under previous chairman, the Fed's future bubbled underground before Volker even arrived:

> In the back rooms of the research division, experimental work with the new science of econometric modeling was going on. This was mind-stretching work for Frank de Leeuw and the rest of the staff involved, and practical benefits did not come quickly. It was not until the decade of the 1970s that the output from econometric models became a really important part of the analytical material that the Board and the Federal Open Market Committee weighed in their deliberations. Such work involved more and more number crunching and was heavily dependent upon the developing computer capability within the staff. (Stockwell 1989, 22)

It is this continued work "in the back rooms" that allowed the Fed to technocratically leap forward under Volcker's leadership.

* * *

With an unconventional methodology in mind, Volcker set his sight on his first target: inflation. Traditional monetary policy uses interest rates to fight inflation by making money, specifically credit, more expensive. While this mechanism is fairly predictable, it is slow, typically taking six months to a year to impact the system. Instead of focusing solely on interest rates, Volker targeted the quantity of money by refusing to inject new capital into the market. Volker's strategy quelled inflation and, at the same time, forced interest rates to rise so that the deflationary pressure persisted. The success of this innovative approach was a testament to the capabilities of the central bank and its firm dedication to fighting inflation (Axilrod 2011a, 92–93).

Although not permanent, this technical shift in policy implementation had a profound impact on the institution. Just as Martin had centralized power through the Board staff, Volcker relied on expert staff to institute a new and untested policy. This policy depended on a seamless transmission of information between the Board in Washington, DC and the personnel at the New York Fed—the acting arm of the strategy. It also relied on popular support, through open communication between the Fed chairman and the public, to avoid political pressure from the Fed's principals. Perhaps most importantly, the success of this new method hinged on the technical capabilities of policymakers, pushing them to be fluent in all the levers of monetary policy—not just the Fed Funds Rate.

* * *

As researchers and Fed veterans can attest, Volcker was a man particularly suited to his position. Former Fed alumnus Stephen Axilrod describes Volcker's abilities:

> He was the essential man for a combination of reasons. He combined great sensitivity to shifting trends in political economy (he could see what the country would now accept) with a willingness to take dramatic action. Moreover, he was technically very competent in the nuts and bolts of monetary policy, which made it easier for the FOMC and the chairman himself to feel confident that the new approach, although not risk free, had a reasonably good chance of working. (Axilrod 2011a, 89)

To uncover the internal Fed dynamics of the "Volcker Revolution," political scientist Cheryl Schonhardt-Bailey and economist Andrew Bailey have reviewed FOMC meeting transcripts from the era. Volcker, they discovered, seamlessly navigated the Fed bureaucracy by utilizing different strategies crafted to each of the various institutional constituencies in order to garner support. When appealing to Board members, Volker's strategy was "repentance": the Fed had to publicly recognize its mistakes and seek to fix them. With the regional bank presidents, Volcker emphasized the need to commit to a particular strategy in order to maintain Fed credibility. And with the staff, Volcker emphasized the need for technical revision—previous models had undervalued the role of the supply of money, and new, more comprehensive models were necessary. A masterful political mover and economic thinker, Volker used a technical "money matters" approach, which became the preeminent method by which the Fed engaged in market behavior between 1979 and 1982 (Bailey and Schonhardt-Bailey 2008).

As political scientist Jack Knott has observed, Volker relied on his technical expertise, connections to the Fed staff, and the centralization of power established by Martin to insure a particular type of data was supplied to policymakers—in essence, leveraging his expertise and connections to the technocratic staff in order to operate as an informational gatekeeper to the FOMC. This use of the staff and data allowed Volcker to build a political coalition within the Fed and outside of it, through public statements that increased the central bank's credibility and put pressure on policymakers to agree with his policy positions (Knott 1986).

Even after the inflation crisis subsided, Volcker sought to increase the role of the staff and the technical nature of monetary policy by further involving the regional bank personnel. In 1983 Volcker introduced the "Summary of Commentary on Current Economic Conditions by Federal Reserve District"—the "Beige Book." The expert staff of each regional bank could now issue a report to the FOMC two weeks prior to meetings, making verbal expression of opinions about regional economic conditions by regional bank presidents obsolete (Federal Open Market Committee 2012). Volcker, once again, had found a way to elevate the role of the technocratic staff and the importance of data above the more pluralist expressions of opinion about economic conditions.

Despite his successes, Paul Volcker was not reappointed again in 1987. By the mid-1980s Volcker began to clash with the supply side ideology of the Reagan Administration, particularly Council of Economic Advisers Chairman Martin Feldstein and subsequent Chairman Beryl Sprinkel. As this ideology pervaded the Treasury and trickle into the Fed through several Reagan Board appointees, conflict mounted over the Fed's role in financial regulation. Administration loyalists sought a deregulated financial marketplace, while Volcker saw a need for continued regulatory action. In fact, Republican Congressman Henry Gonzalez made three separate, failed attempts to impeach Volcker and the entire Federal Reserve Board (Meltzer 2003). Nevertheless, these clashes elevated internal Fed concerns about the growth of their budget and raised fears that they might lose the prized autonomy that had been so crucial to the growth of their technocratic staff.

Three years before his departure, in a prescient speech at the Cosmos Club, Paul Volcker explained, "...the fundamental justification for the structure of the Federal Reserve System is to remove that policy to a degree from the passions of passing politics—politics in the narrow sense—and from electoral considerations" (Volker 1984, 17). Ultimately, it was politics that prevented Volcker from continuing the work toward an increasingly technocratic Fed.

Despite their ideological differences, his successor, noted libertarian economist Alan Greenspan, eagerly continued the trend in technocratic policymaking (Axilrod 2011a).

* * *

Crowding its halls with technically trained economists, adding a vast array of policy tools to its arsenal, and taking on an unprecedented level of regulatory responsibility, the Federal Reserve System was undoubtedly modern, but it was also incredibly complex. These technical developments were only the newest layer of difficulty in an institution already replete with bureaucratic complexities. Involving a convoluted mix of votes from regional bank presidents and Board members, the Fed's policy processes are fraught with procedural intricacies—intricacies that remain unclear to most outsiders. But, as confusing as its processes are, the most complex part of Fed policymaking is the data. Collected from a wide variety of sources and analyzed by both the Board and regional bank staffs, the data is almost impenetrable, rendering any technical justification for a policy decision, to most casual observers, wholly unintelligible. The Fed had become banking's black box, and its mysterious mechanics made outsiders, especially those in Congress, nervous.

The Fed had faced Congressional oversight in the 1970s when its power and efficacy reached opposite ends of the spectrum—oversight manifested in reform and greater demands for transparency. As the years had passed, and the Fed's power, independence, and opacity only increased, so did the need for the central bank to create some method of maintaining this progress while appeasing skeptics ready to curtail their growing prowess. What the Fed needed was a bargaining chip. What the Fed needed was transparency—on their terms.

PART II

Fed Watching: Sentiment Analysis and Data-Driven Investing

5

The Briefcase Watch: Fed Watching at Its Finest?

In the beginning, the Fed was relatively small, and its limited power was dispersed among a network of regional banks bound by regional interests. With different banks setting different rates, savvy investors played the arbitrage game, and the system started to suffer. The banks needed a united front, and they rallied behind the New York Reserve. But a unified system means unified mistakes. New York failed to interpret the market correctly, and their mistake was compounded across the entire system. The stock market crashed, banks failed, and the country fell into a Great Depression. With an economy collapsing around it, the Fed held steady, letting banks go under and sticking to gold. The strategy paid off in the long run, but the Fed paid for it in the meantime.

The New Deal meant a new set of masters for the central bank, and the Federal Reserve System was locked in a battle for independence that would last two decades. The Fed achieved independence in the early 1950s, and the chairmanship of Martin brought a focus and purpose to the dispersed system of Federal Reserve banks. The Fed evolved, consolidating power in the Board and voices into data. But after 20 years, Martin left—taking progress with him. Under Burns and Miller the Fed lost its way—prompting an all-too-eager Congress to step in, impose reforms and demand transparency.

It did not take long, however, for the Fed to find its footing. When Volcker took the helm, he continued the mechanistic march Martin had started. The Beige Book joined the blue and green tomes, data-driven methodologies became standard practice, and an increasingly educated staff manned the monetary levers. The central bank grew ever more independent, centralized, and technocratic. It grew more powerful, too.

* * *

When Alan Greenspan took the wheel, the central banking system that started in the mind of one politician was not fully grasped by many others. Banking, even at a basic level, is not the most popular topic: introduce finance into a casual conversation and eyes glaze over. But the Federal Reserve was far from basic level banking. The budding system had become a full-fledged technocratic leviathan, and Greenspan did not break that trend. Technocratic growth and decision making bloomed under his watch, and it became clear that just as Arthur Burns experienced a backlash in the 1970s over centralization and faulty policy, Greenspan could face a similar reaction in the 1990s, but for different reasons: the increasing technocracy of the central bank. The Federal Reserve was just too big, too powerful, and too confusing to remain as it was—and so a backlash loomed. It was in this era, after years of enigmatic existence, that the Fed finally begins to let in a little light. This chapter covers the beginnings of the era of the transparent Fed and the interpretive analyses that have arisen out of this policy transparency.

Long before Greenspan began implementing transparency measures, Volcker, the prescient intellect he was, discussed the delicate balance the Fed would have to maintain to when implementing disclosure in Reserve operations:

> Sunshine may at times be a healthy and essential antidote to festering sores. But, carried to excess, I have seen it wilt some tender plants that need quiet cultivation. Sometimes, when legitimate efforts to reach reconciliation will be interpreted as public defeat or "selling out," it seems to have the practical effect of simply hardening antagonistic positions. (Volker 1984, 10)

Transparency is a double-edged sword, to be wielded with care. Disclose too little, and one can invite criticism, outside control and "festering sores"; disclose too much, and one can prevent a complex process from working as it should. But, tricky as it was, transparency would become an integral part of central banking policy—not only in the American system, but around the world.

* * *

Mired in confusion and speculation about the Fed's role in the economy, Greenspan-era skeptics began a public campaign to shed sunlight on the Fed. The "briefcase watch" was an early, unintentional—and rather whimsical—part of this campaign. On the morning of a Federal Open Market Committee (FOMC) meeting, reporters would hound Greenspan, desperate to get a glimpse of his briefcase. The briefcase's dimensions, it was speculated, could hold the key to the Fed's next moves: a thin briefcase was thought to mean Greenspan had not been reviewing the data, and the fed funds rate—the interest rate on overnight loans between banks—would stay put; a thick briefcase meant that a diligent Greenspan had been at work reviewing data and intended to change rates.

Silly as it was, the "briefcase watch" was a telling development. The Fed had become so important to the financial world that even speculative information on its plans was newsworthy. While illustrating the ascendancy of the Fed, the "briefcase watch" also demonstrated how little information was available on central banking operations: if the width of a briefcase merited airtime and print media coverage, then clearly investors and analysts were starved for information. For the level of influence the Fed wielded over the economic machine, the level of secrecy it was allowed to maintain over its processes seems quite remarkable. As the public scrutiny over the mysterious institution mounted, Greenspan, unlike Burns, opted to move before Congress elected to act. He provided a small amount of transparency.

Beginning in 1994, the Fed released statements regarding changes to the overnight Fed Funds Rate. By 1998, these press releases were issued at the conclusion of each FOMC meeting, even if rates remained unchanged (Crosse and Paschal 2012). While novel in the United States, such policy was not the Fed's innovation. These transparency measures were part of a global movement the Fed was joining as central banks around the world pursued new communication methods. This widespread adoption of central bank transparency was based partly on an idea derived from rational expectations philosophy about the utility of open communication: transparency could potentially help manage market expectations about economic performance—thereby working to minimize economic shocks (The Federal Reserve Bank of Minneapolis 2015).

It is important to note that transparency is not equivalent to representation, but as the Fed released more information concerning its plans, public perception of the institution—particularly the Fed chairman—changed. Popular opinion and market actors adapted to the new resource, and the news media latched onto the storyline that Fed communications impact markets.

* * *

Despite, or possibly because of, these transparency measures, Fed watching after the briefcase watch only became more intense. As the Fed released more information and officials spoke more regularly, reporters, forecasters, and financial analysts increased their efforts to scour Fed communications in an attempt to glean some indication about the central bank's future policy steps. The persistent belief among these Fed watchers was that the information conveyed by Fed officials provided a credible signal about future policy. This belief remained despite the fact that Fed officials were known to have developed their own linguistic style to hide information—a language that came to be known as "Fedspeak."

In "How Do Central Banks Talk?," Princeton Economist Alan Blinder and his coauthors explain the history of the Fed's language of concealment:

> The Fed has been traditionally portrayed as tight-lipped, secretive, and cryptic. Arthur Burns and Paul Volker, its chairman for most of the 1970s and 1980s, were famous for blowing smoke—both literally and figuratively—when they appeared before Congress, and on other occasions as well. Each of them spoke a turgid dialect of English that came to be known as "Fedspeak," a term which seems to connote the use of numerous and complicated words to convey little if any meaning. As chairman since 1987, Alan Greenspan is credited with raising Fedspeak to a high art. He used to take pride in the resulting obfuscation—even characterizing his own way of communications as "mumbling with great incoherence." In a famous incident, he once told a US senator, who claimed to have understood what

the famous obscurantist chairman had just said, that "in that case, I must have misspoken." (Blinder et al. 2001, 66)

Straddling the delicate line created by transparency, Greenspan used Fedspeak to calm market reactions to Fed policy (Leonard and Coy 2012). While Fedspeak was originally a tool of obfuscation, Greenspan gradually changed his intent from confusion to, at least, some level of clarity (Blinder et al. 2001). And "the markets," Blinder and his coauthors remark, "seem to be getting the message" (Blinder et al. 2001).

Greenspan's successors have continued this trend. In 2011, indicating another step toward open communication, the Ben Bernanke-led Fed began giving press conferences—giving investors and analysts access to unprecedented amounts of information. In recent speeches, current chairman Janet Yellen has even gone so far as to say "communications are policy" in reference to forward guidance (Yellen 2013). With forward guidance, the Federal Reserve website explains, "The Federal Open Market Committee provides an indication to households, businesses, and investors about the stance of monetary policy expected to prevail in the future" (Board of Governors of the Federal Reserve System 2015a). Fed personnel have spoken out as well, strengthening the ties between word and deed. In 2012, for instance, Fed Board Governor Jeremy Stein spoke about the value of open communication—specifically as it directly relates to future monetary policy moves:

> I believe that the LSAP component of the statement helped bolster the credibility of the forward guidance component by pairing a declaration about future intentions with an immediate and concrete set of actions. And I suspect that this complementarity helps explain the strong positive reaction of the stock market to the release of the statement. In addition to this signaling channel. (Stein 2012)

As the Fed increases its use of open communication, the line between communication and action continues to blur, until, as Yellen stated, communications have become policy.

On a global scale, it is becoming increasingly clear that words are action. The Swiss National Bank, for instance, caused panic in the markets within minutes of announcing the elimination of their exchange rate peg. The Swiss franc moved 20 percent in a single day before the central bank implemented any substantive change in monetary policy. While it had not implemented policy in the traditional sense, it had employed another market-moving tool: transparent communication.

* * *

Domestically and globally, words and policy have become intermingled, and the trend, it seems, will only continue toward more clear, open communication—meaning, of course, words will have greater power in the economy:

> The bad old days of central bank mystique are over. All central banks evolve, however grudgingly, towards more transparency and greater communication. The process, which reflects trends in other aspects of public life wholly apart from central banking, is far from over. Some central banks may still believe that they can retain secrecy in particular areas (e.g. their forecasts, the substance of their internal deliberations, the models they use) indefinitely. But we are skeptical. Other central banks are acting as pioneers and showing, along the way, not only that transparency does not hurt, but that it increases the efficiency of monetary policy and enhances credibility, independence and public support. (Blinder et al. 2001, 92)

Transparency is central bank policy, and, consequently, understanding central bank language is a prerequisite for understanding central banking—and the economy as a whole.

With information pouring in from multiple streams, the task of objectively interpreting has become daunting. Financial analysts carefully examine central bank communications, but unfortunately, their current approach fails to consider many vital aspects of the available data and statements. Stateside, the interpretation of central bank communication has become much like the literary practice of close reading. In literary studies, it is common practice to draw sweeping interpretations from the granular details of a poem or short story. For example, if an author used "devoured" instead of "consumed" to describe the actions of character, a literary critic could use this subtle detail, along with a handful of others, to support an animalistic reading of an entire piece. In the same way—rather than employing expansive interpretation that takes into account the whole breadth of what is now available—modern Fed watching has become fixated on deriving significant meaning from single words or phrases. A March 2015 article in the *New York Times* provides a perfect example of this laser focus on individual terms, rather than the entire text, spending thousands of words and calling on an entourage of experts to elaborate on the Fed's use of the word "patient" in their communications (Stewart 2015).

With Fed press releases, this practice makes some sense. The language used is remarkably consistent, and the slightest change in verbiage could have dramatic implications on the Fed's current views and plans. Updates to press releases are particularly conspicuous because the texts are altered through track changes—a method that lends itself to detail-centric interpretation. Despite this consistency, the methodology falls prey to human error. While small deviations could have significance, subjective analysis leaves the door open for overreaction. It is incredibly difficult for individual analysts judging minute changes in a specific press release to objectively consider historical patterns and make a smart, evidence-based prediction of what the Fed will do. The presence of any overreactions in their interpretation, of course, has the potential to powerfully alter the intended meaning of the text. But this is the best-case scenario for current techniques. This method has carried over to minutes, speeches, and other crucial central bank communications, and even other central banks that do not use track changes at all, which means Fed watchers are skipping over vital, market-moving information. Although analysts have far more information than they did when some of their best leads lay in the width of a briefcase, their techniques have not progressed as much the central bank communications have.

* * *

The history of the Federal Reserve is a story of evolution, and transparency is just the latest development. Since the financial crisis, central bankers—struggling to head off criticism—have adopted increasingly transparent policy; the result has been central bankers constantly declaring the importance of communications to the public—a trend that is particularly obvious in the Federal Reserve.

With Ben Bernanke instituting press conferences and Janet Yellen directly telling audiences that communications are policy (Yellen 2013), it is clear that a new era of central banking has arrived, an era where transparent communications are just as important as direct quantitative policy action.

Unfortunately, analysis of central banking has not kept pace with the evolution of the institution it seeks to illuminate. Putting a crack in its legacy of opacity, the Federal Reserve now presents the financial world with a wealth of information; Congressional testimony, press conferences, meeting minutes, press releases are all easily accessible—but are evaluated using techniques that focus on details at the expense of the larger available context. In other words, current practices cannot see the forest for the trees—despite the fact that the mass adoption of transparency among the central banking community has made, for the first time, seeing the forest feasible. In a financial world that is increasingly impacted by central bank policy, accurate interpretation of communications has become more vital—and more valuable—than ever before.

6

Data-Driven Fed Watching: Comprehensive, Unbiased, and Quantitative

The days of an unknowable Fed are over. Advisors, financiers, and financial professionals of all levels no longer need to speculate about the width of a briefcase or spend valuable hours teasing apart elusive—or perhaps nonexistent—kernels of policy embedded in Fedspeak. The Fed has embraced transparency, and the financial world is better for it. But, the abundance of central banking data now available to financial professionals does not do much good unless accompanied by effective analysis. Current Fed watching certainly supplies abundant analysis—and has even created a rigorous approach to press release interpretation—but the overall effectiveness of this methodology is questionable in a world where central banks use multiple important lines of communication. Even at their best, modern methods provide projections based on qualitative opinions—not quantitative data—when identifying the Fed's current policy position. Current Fed watching techniques simply do not provide the strongest analysis of the Fed's outlook and future policy for financial professionals. If an accurate assessment of central bank communication is important to understanding the market—and it undoubtedly is—analysts ought to stop treating central bank communications like poetry when attempting to zero in on policy: "close reading" may be great for unlocking Shakespeare's sonnets, but it's not the best method of understanding essential, market-moving data. This chapter tackles the serious question facing investors, portfolio managers, and anyone else for whom the Fed's policy is vital information: In the modern era of the Fed transparency, what is the best means of interpreting central bank communications?

* * *

To fully realize the potential of the data available, financial professionals need analytics—but not all analytics are created equal. In the current climate of big data and analytic super tools, it can be difficult to separate the wheat from the chaff. As Harvard professor and director of the Institute for Quantitative Social Science Gary King can attest, even experts can overlook the biggest methodological errors. When these experts, according to Professor King, wanted to put big data to work to help forecast unemployment, they chose to tap social media. By keeping track of words like "jobs" and "classifieds" in the Twittersphere and beyond, the group hoped to discover a relationship between the monthly unemployment rate and the tagged terms. As research progressed, there was a huge jump in the one of the key terms—"jobs"—potentially signalling a dramatic uptick in unemployment. At least, that was the hypothesis. Instead of serving as a tool of prediction, the method, as it turns out, had only echoed front-page news—entirely unrelated news at that. "What they hadn't noticed," Gary King explains, "was Steve Jobs died" (Armerding 2013). The innovator's unfortunate departure was responsible for the jump in the key term, not any coming wave of unemployment. The lesson is clear: a wealth of data coupled with cutting-edge methods don't necessarily equal success. It is easy to get swept up in the latest technological trends without applying appropriate, detailed scrutiny—and many have fallen prey to the promise of analytics without taking a closer look under the hood.

* * *

What is needed is a new method of Fed watching: an interpretive technique that draws upon expert judgment while minimizing the human errors that mark current practices, one that leverages the advantages of analytics without falling prey to unsound methodology. Seeing this need, we developed a better means of textual analysis. Drawing on literature across the social sciences, statistics, data science, and computing, we have developed a process—under the company Prattle—engineered to navigate these challenges and produce comprehensive, unbiased, and quantitative analysis of vital, market-moving central bank texts.

The process begins with a foundation of reference texts. These texts are central bank communications that have led to discrete, identifiable market reactions, and the type and intensity of these market reactions allow the texts to be scored by those with adequate expertise. For central banks, this score is an indication of the "hawkishness" or "dovishness" of a central bank's position on the economy. A hawkish central bank views the economy as strong and growing and, because of this perception, will soon implement contractionary monetary policy—raising interest rates to insure credit is less available—in an attempt to keep the market from overheating. A dovish central bank believes the economy is struggling and takes the corresponding strategy: lowering interest rates to encourage growth through a climate of easier access to credit. Directly connected to varying degrees of market reaction, these reference documents are firmly rooted in history—making them an excellent foundation for comparison.

Using these reference texts, we have been able to reliably correlate specific words, phrases, sentences, paragraphs, and whole communications to market reactions. This is possible, in part, because the Fed has an established lexicon. The deliberate nature of their communication habits means that the communications themselves can be evaluated based on the reactions they have historically elicited since transparency has become a significant component of Fed policy. In this case, the institutional transition toward transparency during the mid-to-late 1990s means that Fed communications beginning in 1998 meet the necessary conditions for our purposes. Using our domain expertise, we have ordinally ranked not just words, but also phrases, sentences, paragraphs, and entire communications as positive or negative based on nature of the reaction incited. Terminology linked to hawkish policy and corresponding market reaction is awarded positive numbers based on the level of the response. Conversely, dovish terms are awarded negative numbers. This lexicon of hawkish and dovish terminology is the backbone of the process.

Provided with this context, it now becomes possible to accurately evaluate current central bank communications. Aggregating text from all the streams of Fed communication within the desired timeframe, our process then generates a score for the sample in light of the pool of hawkish and dovish communications. The score generated is the average rating of all the hawkish and dovish expressions embedded within the selected documents. This method allows Prattle to generate the Fed's "mood"—their current position on the economy, and their inflation expectations specifically, relative to an established history of communications and market reactions. The outcome of this entire process is the Fed Index, the only comprehensive, unbiased, and quantitative data analysis method in existence on the central bank's economic outlook.

* * *

It is important to note that our analytical process differs significantly from the methods employed by standard automated interpretation processes known as sentiment analysis. Like our method, sentiment analysis produces a quantitative assessment, but it does so in a distinctly different manner. Generalized sentiment analysis commonly works by first predefining a list of positive and negative buzzwords, then subtracting the sum value of the negative buzzwords that appear in a given text from the positive buzzwords. In more sophisticated iterations of sentiment analysis, whole phrases are included in a dictionary of buzz terms and are used in the scoring of texts. But the application of either of these versions of sentiment analysis to Fed communications would be inappropriate because of the method by which the list of buzz terms is created. The production of the set of term values is not only subject to selection bias, but it is often carried out by those lacking the subject-matter expertise to properly identify and rank the terms. Given the esoteric and constantly evolving nature of Fed communications, it is clear that any program built to interpret these texts would need a high level of fluency and objectivity to create scientifically valid assessments.

Instead of selecting and predefining the lexicon that we use as a basis of evaluation, we generate values through an algorithmic assessment of the central bank terminology's actual connection to market reaction. Using our domain expertise, whole documents are paired with the market reactions they elicited. After this an automated analytical process evaluates these documents' relationships to the separate market reactions they individually elicit. Then, the scores of each word, phrase, sentence, and paragraph of these communications that have bearing on the market are produced according to their actual relationship to financial fluctuations. As more documents are analyzed, the texts are more accurately oriented to one another and, consequently, the relative values of each expression become increasingly accurate. By utilizing our subject-matter expertise to make broad connections between the documents and the market, and using an automated process to identify the natural connections that emerge between specific expressions and the market, our methodology leverages the deep domain expertise provided by economists and the speed and objectivity afforded by automation.

* * *

While holding an edge over generalized sentiment analysis, this process also has several distinct advantages over current Fed watching methods.

Instead of viewing a text, or only specific words within a text, apart from other relevant streams, our score is derived from the totality of the Fed's public discourse. By relying on the entire scope of what is available, our inherently comprehensive methodology is entirely free from selection bias—a methodological drawback of not only the buzzword-based approach to sentiment analysis discussed above, but orthodox Fed watching as well. When selecting texts or key terms, analysts, whether they are aware of it or not, are inevitably influenced by past experiences or underlying—possibly underhanded—ulterior motives. These influences translate into undue analytical attention toward specific texts and words, skewing the accuracy of the interpretation. By remaining indiscriminate and inclusive, our process systematically hedges against this bias. The inclusivity of the process also allows it to make a far more credible claim to being an accurate (and precise) estimation of the Fed's current position. Individual communications are inherently incomplete, meaning that any analysis derived from just one source, even a few sources, clearly has less claim on reflecting the position of the institution than an analysis based on the sum of all available sources.

This diagnosis is not meant to fault modern analysts for their selectivity. Given the sheer volume of communication output across all the Fed's channels, it would be infeasible for individual analysts to simultaneously keep in mind all current Fed communications when giving their assessment. Humans can only handle so much bandwidth, as it were, and this cognitive limitation makes selectivity the best means of securing higher-quality analysis. Our process, however, has no such limitation.

The strength of our methodology compared to traditional Fed watching practices is further bolstered by its objective scoring process. It is incredibly challenging for Fed watchers to evaluate central bank communications with respect to an accurate, historical representation of what specific words mean. Just like with document selection, any number of irrelevant influences and human errors can come into play during textual interpretation. An analyst could have a momentary mental lapse, could have just had an argument with a spouse, or could have an upset stomach. An analyst could have ulterior motives for desiring a certain Fed text to be understood by the market in a particular way, or could be swayed by unknown political purposes. In any case, human interpretation is constantly subject to a variety of impulses, moods, and errors; and in the financial world, such biases can easily translate into seriously flawed business decisions. Our system removes these possibilities from the interpretive process. By grounding every score in historical, causally connected market reactions, our process makes sure the only source for each interpretation is the breadth of available evidence.

* * *

The Fed Index is not the only source of quantitative analysis of the Fed. By predicting the date that the Fed will raise rates, traditional Fed watching also produces its own quantitative data from the central bank's communications. However, our methodology is the only source of a quantified assessment of the central bank's current position. Contemporary Fed watchers write qualitative appraisals of the Fed's disposition and then follow that assessment with an associated projection. Qualitative assessments are, however, inherently difficult to pinpoint. Phrases like "very hawkish" or "fairly dovish," for example, can give a reader a general feel for the Fed's attitude, but that reader can only evaluate those descriptions in light of their own understanding of "hawkish" and "dovish"—as well as "very" and "fairly." This interpretive dilemma means a plurality of Fed moods can be derived from the same words by different readers. When it comes to generating investment strategies in light of such qualitative assessments, the incorporation of these interpretations is more art than science—leaving substantial room for error. By assigning the Fed's current mood a specific numerical value relative to previous communication, our process gives a discrete value to textual data, removing the ambiguity qualitative assessments allow for. How hawkish is "very hawkish"? Who knows? But 1.5 hawkish on a scale of negative 2 to 2 offers a more precise picture of the Fed's outlook.

* * *

While the comprehensive, unbiased, and quantitative data our method produces represents the frontier of Fed watching, there are two additional advantages that merit discussion.

The scoring process itself is very rapid, assessing a text in as little as seven to ten seconds. By comparison, an analyst using traditional methods could conceivably read and write a response to a communication in 15 or more minutes, which, in the world of quantitative finance, is a lifetime. Speed, as MIT Professor Kevin Slavin notes, is everything in business:

> The algorithms of Wall Street are dependent on one quality above all else, which is speed. And they operate on milliseconds and microseconds. And just to give you a sense of what microseconds are, it takes you 500,000 microseconds just to click a mouse. But if you're a Wall Street algorithm and you're 5 microseconds behind, you're a loser. So if you were an algorithm, you'd look for an architect like the one that I met in Frankfurt who was hollowing out a skyscraper—throwing out all the furniture, all the infrastructure for human use and just running steel on the floors to get ready for the stacks of servers to go in—all so that an algorithm could get close to the Internet. (Slavin 2015)

If gutting a skyscraper sounds like an extreme measure to gain a handful of microseconds on the competition, Slavin follows this example with an even more dramatic case, further emphasizing the primacy of speed in trade:

> And you think of the Internet as this kind of distributed system—and of course it is—but it's distributed from places, right? In New York, this is where it's distributed from—the Carrier Hotel, located on Hudson Street. And this is really where the wires come right up into the city. And the reality is that the further away you are from that, you're a few microseconds behind. But if you zoom out, you would see an 825-mile trench between New York City and Chicago. It's been built over the last few years by a company called Spread Networks. This is a fiber-optic cable that was laid between those two cities to just be able to traffic one signal 37 times faster than you can click a mouse—just for these algorithms. And when you think about this, that we're running through the United States with dynamite and rock saws so that an algorithm can close the deal 3 microseconds faster. (Slavin 2015)

As enormous as the gap between 15 minutes and 10 seconds is, that is the best-case scenario for traditional methods: most analyses are published hours or even days after the communication is released. Additionally, unlike human analysis, which tends to decline in quality as the amount of available time decreases, the scores produced by our methodology are always the product of the spectrum of available evidence. This means that our methodology provides not only speed, but smart speed as well.

The second advantage is the ease with which Fed Index data can be integrated into existing financial models. As mentioned earlier, qualitative assessments are necessarily resistant to specificity. Unfortunately for finance professionals, this lack of specificity translates into a lack of usability when it comes to financial modeling. "Very hawkish" just isn't a very useful input. A concrete number, however, is far easier to handle: quantitative data is a natural fit for existing multifactor investment models. This ease of integration means money saved. And, as opposed to qualitative assessments, our data allows financial professionals to accurately estimate how much of a dollar difference our information will actually make.

Another salient point concerning investment model integration is the unique nature of our data. Our data demonstrates a very low correlation to other data streams used as inputs for multifactor investment models, which indicates that our methodology captures novel economic cues not accounted for by other analytics. Not only is this a guarantee of low redundancy when our data is included in such models, but it would also strongly suggest that the resulting projections would have improved accuracy.

With unique, evidence-based evaluations generated at a blistering pace and integrated directly into their financial models, users can make the most informed decisions possible on the Fed's market-moving policies, and they can do so more quickly and effectively than those reliant on traditional methods. This allows users to avoid the losses that can result from delayed analysis. In other words, instant data means that users know the precise position of the Fed at that very moment—allowing for the best moves—while standard practice would necessitate post hoc hedging: corrective financial moves made in light of new information. By eliminating the need for post hoc hedging, our data enables financial professionals to actually trust their models—even when central bankers are making market-moving policy statements.

* * *

As the Fed has ramped up its transparency efforts, pushing out more data through more channels than ever before, it has become increasingly difficult to offer accurate, comprehensive assessments of its economic position through traditional, qualitative methods. The central bank's current communicative practices present traditional Fed watchers with an unprecedented task, requiring unprecedented analytical tools. All its aspects considered, our process offers a suite of features that push Fed watching into the digital age. Rooted in history, unfettered by bias and offering clear, measurable appraisals based on comprehensive examination of historical and current Fed documents, the Fed Index keeps stride with the ascendant central bank that has emerged since the financial crisis: a central bank that does far more than set the discount rate. The modern Fed influences all facets of the economy, and those with any interest in succeeding as an investor cannot afford anything less than the best data on the biggest market mover of them all, the Federal Reserve.

7

Fixed-Income Investing: Fed Sentiment Drives Bonds

The Fed and fixed-income investments have a long history: buying and selling bonds and bills to maintain the price of money is a traditional domain of the Fed. Through wars and financial crises, the central bank and this market have forged a deep connection, and, with this history, it's no wonder that when the Fed speaks its words ripple across the fixed-income markets.

The undisputed market heavyweight, the central bank's role in fixed income is essential for market players to understand, and its actions, now conflated with its words, are the fundamental driver of trade. This chapter begins by reviewing the fundamentals of the market—bonds, bills, and general fixed-income trade—and then shifts to a discussion of our work interpreting Fed communications and its relevance to the study of this nuanced market, particularly Treasury bonds. This relevance is investigated through a pair of compelling analyses. First, we examine a backtest performed with a fixed-income portfolio that was managed using our Fed sentiment data—and only that data—as the trade signal. Then a more comprehensive perspective is offered, analyzing how our signal, which is an interpretation of Fed communications, can be compared to the Fed's action, using the federal funds rate (FFR) as an economic barometer. The notable performance of this portfolio and the strong relationship between our data and the bond market are two more testaments to the power the central bank's language wields over fixed-income markets.

* * *

Fixed income is a term used for a security that gives the investor a regular income on fixed terms. Generally, there are a few types of fixed-income securities: government bonds, municipal (local government) bonds, and corporate bonds. In essence, they all take the form of a loan. Essentially, an investor, in the form of a bond purchase, allows the seller to borrow money, and the seller agrees to pay the investor back at some later date, either in lump sum or a series of payments. This series of (interest) payments is known as coupon payments. Shorter-term bonds, frequently referred to as bills, rarely have coupon payments, while longer-term bonds almost always do.

There are two separate markets for debt in these forms. The first is the primary market, where purchasers can buy debt directly from the original seller. An investor can, in fact, directly buy government bonds from the US Treasury—as well as most other debt issuers. A significant portion of the fixed-income market is directly invested as debt holders for a variety of actors.

Next is the secondary bond market. In this space, bonds purchased on the primary market are resold. Investors, desiring a return on their investment sooner than the bond's maturity, seek fair market value for the asset they currently hold. Naturally, since the face value of the bond is guaranteed, investors can, with minimal risk (Greece is a recent exception), see returns in the secondary market. And also, since this guarantee is in place, bonds are easily sold and resold many times (Greece is an example of an exception to this rule here as well). This ease of convertibility to and from cash makes bonds a liquid asset.

While fixed income is now one of the lowest growth areas of investment, it is also, by design, the lowest risk—if the bond issuer is stable. Strictly holding onto long-term bonds is theoretically a no-risk investment—only in the case of government or corporate default, or debt restructuring, is the investment in real trouble. As a concept, fixed income is rather simple, but these simple mechanics regulate an enormous amount of wealth: literally trillions of dollars are regularly at stake in this market. Because the stakes are so high, even minor shifts have outsized consequences: movements in a hundredth of a percent can be the difference between success and failure. A multitude of influences play into market shifts, but in this space, the Federal Reserve's decisive role deserves and receives more attention than any other factor.

* * *

In order to comprehensively backtest fixed income, we've decided to use an ETF—an exchange-traded fund. ETFs operate much like a stock on the open market. They are also backed by a specific set of securities, like government bonds, and generally are, in comparison to normal bonds, a riskier investment. But, since the underlying asset is very low risk, ETFs based on bonds are typically less prone to extreme volatility and commonly represent good "buy-and-hold" opportunities.

We have also chosen to use an ETF instead of, for instance, the bond price on the secondary market on an exchange for reasons of mathematical clarity. There are many complexities to buying and selling bonds on the secondary market—like the synthetic nature of price for any given security or the difficulty of tracking coupon payments—and these intricacies make for a poor test candidate. The ETF effectively captures much of the underlying information contained in the price movements of the securities and, therefore, represents a solid asset to test. The specific ETF we used for our backtesting is the iShares 20+ Year Treasury ETF (ticker symbol TLT), and it is indexed to 20- and 30-year US Treasury bonds.

The backtest works as a full paper-trading example from 2004 to 2014. By paper trading, we mean that the example only considers data prior to the start of 2004 as we make our first trading decision in 2004. As we move forward, we update our information about the basic parameters between the Fed Index data and the price levels of the ETF. In short, each day's trade is only informed by the data that would have been available to us on that day. The simulation progresses through this 10-year span. After making the initial investment decision, we take either a long or short position. There is no cash withholding, and we assume there are no transaction costs (in a highly liquid ETF like the TLT, transaction costs are usually quite low). Additionally, this test is performed daily. We take one (and only one) position each day.

Long positions imply we are simply buying the asset and holding on to it as (hopefully) it increases in value. Short positions are the opposite. We actually take out a short-term loan, paid back in the asset itself, and hold on to cash as we wait (again, hopefully) for the asset to drop in value. After the price lowers, we buy the asset at a now lower price than we sold it for, and pay back the original loan in the shares of the asset that we now temporarily possess.

The data used was our own proprietary Fed watching data (Fed Index), and the price and dividend information on the TLT from Yahoo Finance for the entire history of the ETF, which had a date of inception on July 22, 2002. The data prior to the start date of the paper-trading simulation is used to calculate parameters relevant to the backtest, such as the optimal lag structure (which is how far back we look at our data to consider the trading decision made on any given day) for the Fed Index and trading thresholds. Specifically, the data used is the daily close price of the TLT.

We use a fairly simple momentum-based strategy to make trading decisions. Generally put, we look at a moving average of the Fed Index, and, if we detect a significant upward or downward trend, we take a long or short position, respectively. More formally, we are looking at a moving average of the price level, and, considering the average deviation from the moving average, if we detect a large enough change in the numeric derivative across time, we reconsider our position. If we detect a large upward shift, for example, and are already in a long position, we do not change. On the other hand, if we are long and detect a downward shift, we move to a short position. These are the basics of our backtesting settings, but the entire process merits a more detailed explanation.

* * *

The Fed Index in its raw form is simply a collection of scores attached to information released at specific times, and these scores are not necessarily released on consecutive days. In order to calculate the daily value of the signal, we have to transform the scores.

First, we average communications on a daily level. While there are days without communications, there are also days with multiple communications. In order to consider the position of the Fed in between communications, we perform a linear approximation between communications. A line is drawn from one communication to the next, and the value of that line on a day without a communication is recorded. This is because we believe that the unofficial policy position of the Fed on any given day is actually a bargain between all the institution's relevant decision makers. Given this, the policy the Fed is likely to choose at any moment is actually located within the space defined by outlying hawkish and dovish scores in any stretch of time. A common alternative to linear approximation when constructing signals such as this is to carry forward the last nonmissing value, but we have found that this leads to an inaccurate portrayal of the real flow of the Fed's policy orientation across time.

Next, the optimal level of correlation between the pretest—and, as the simulation progresses, previous test—data is used to find the exact number of days the Fed Index should be lagged to optimize the correlation between the TLT and the Fed Index. In both pretest and progressing data, we found that the highest level of correlation occurs at 193 days. This lag is consistent with conventional monetary economics, which states that markets take at least six months to react to monetary policy. In this case we found that the markets take just over six months to appropriately react. Given this lag structure, we only made trading decisions on information released 193 days before the date of the simulation trade day. That is, only if a communication occurred on that date, do we consider making a trade.

After lagging the data, we calculate a moving average—and this is recalculated for every day of the study. This averaging is necessary to convert the Fed Index into a smooth, readable signal. Without averaging, the lines connecting the scattered Fed Index values create a chaotic landscape, dipping and diving among the disparate values. By means of a ten-day moving average, this data is reduced to a smooth slope. The score for any given day then becomes the average of the last ten days, and this average is calculated daily, moving with each trade day.

Finally, we calculate the daily momentum of the signal. The momentum is the direction of the signal. This direction is the difference between the value of the smoothed average of the signal at the beginning of the day and the value of the smoothed average of the signal at the end of the day. If this difference begins to change dramatically, we know that the mood of the Fed is beginning to shift. (Remember, the mood that informs our trading positions is actually the position of the Fed 193 days before the trading day.) By examining the history of the signal, we were able to determine what indicates a shift in momentum by first determining what the average rate of change in the ascent (towards hawkish) or descent (towards dovish) of the Fed Index was. We then noted the range of rates of change that consistently signalled a significant shift in momentum. The thresholds of these rates of change were on the far low and high ends of the rate of change values—in the bottom and top quintiles (20 and 80 percent to be exact)—and these thresholds informed our trading decisions. If the Fed Index's momentum passed these thresholds, we changed positions; if it stayed within them, we held our position. The criteria for what constitutes a threshold was also constantly updated as our data on the Fed's sentiment continued to pour in. This allowed our understanding of the attitude shifts in the Fed to become, at least in theory, increasingly accurate, which, in turn, translated to better trading decisions as time passed.

* * *

The results of our backtesting, using only the Fed Index as the trading signal, were extremely positive. With an initial investment of 100,000 dollars, our simulated portfolio grew significantly, landing at a final value of 157,911 dollars on December 31, 2014—representing a 8,788 dollar alpha over a control buy-and-hold portfolio.

Over the course of the 12-year trading period, 127 positions were taken, with an average of just over 16 days per position. Guided by the central banking sentiment, the portfolio was able to navigate the tremendous pitfalls of the financial crisis—avoiding the severe losses suffered by nearly every market index and trading strategy. It is remarkable that this level of performance (see Figure 7.1) was possible given the simplicity of our trading model, but it speaks to

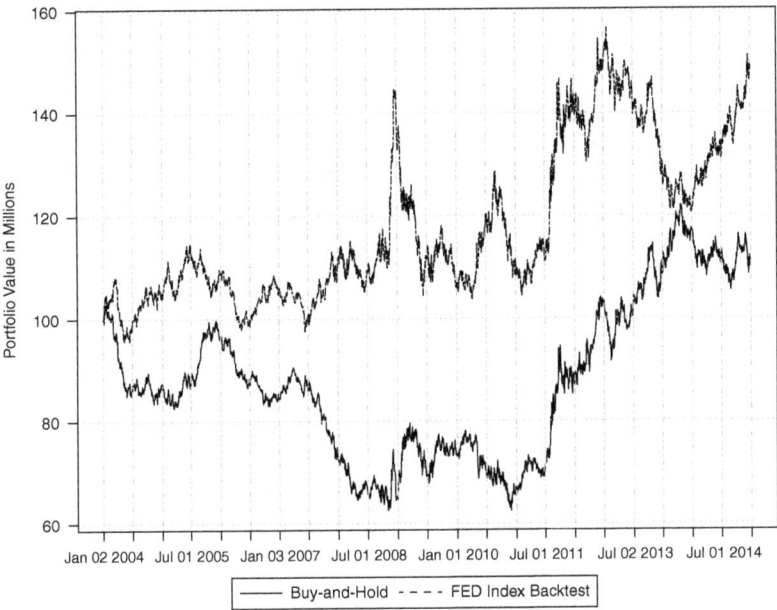

Figure 7.1 Performance of a Fed Index-driven simulated portfolio.

the increasing power of the Fed's word—both as a predictive text and a market mover.

* * *

As the reliable performance of the backtested portfolio would suggest, there seems to be a significant relationship between the Fed Index and this market. Figure 7.2 illustrates how closely our Fed sentiment data is correlated to fixed-income pricing from 1998 to 2012.

The correlation between the Fed Index and the ten-year Treasury bond—a market benchmark—is noticeably greater than the correlation between the FFR and the ten-year bond. At no time is this disparity more obvious than since the financial crisis: since the recession, the FFR has been pinned to the zero, effectively decoupling it from the treasury; the Fed Index, on the other hand, has continued to oscillate in tandem with the bond. This development reinforces the importance of the Fed's official

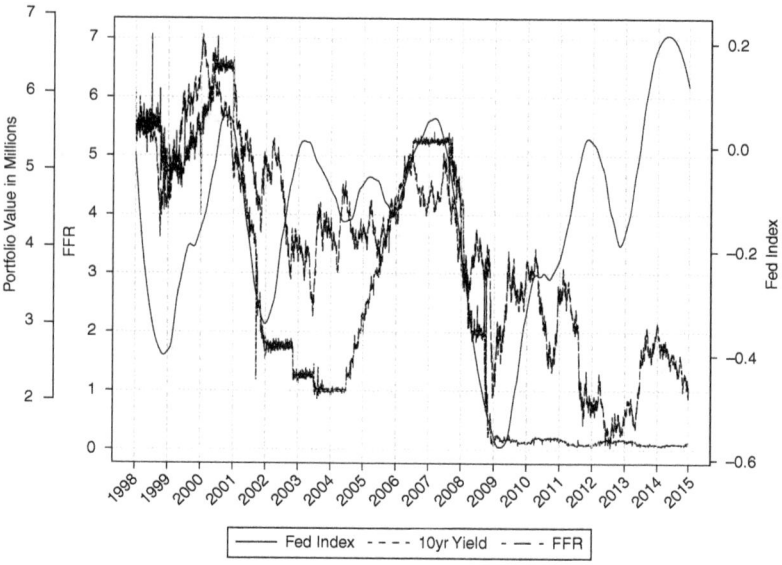

Figure 7.2 Fed Index, FFR, and a ten-year bond yield.

communications regarding the economy, as opposed to its actions. The FFR is recognized as a standard lever of economic control, and its manipulation is a direct demonstration of central bank action. Transparency, as this book has chronicled, is a relatively recent development, and, in comparison to directly implemented policy, the relationship between it and market action might seem less consequential. Figure 7.2 paints runs contrary to expectations, portraying a market moved more by word than by deed. The data only reinforces what Janet Yellen has been telling Fed watchers: in the modern era of central banking, "communications are policy" (Yellen 2013).

But Fed communications do not only impact the market; they also reveal trends that most investors could not see in advance. Fed policymakers are privy to a wide variety of macroeconomic information—far beyond that which most market actors have access to. The Fed communications are, therefore, an indicator for a wide variety of macromarket drivers in addition to Fed policy itself. Given this relationship to coming trends, central bank sentiment, interpreted properly, would be expected to serve as an excellent predictor. And with the Fed Index, that is exactly what is seen: in the majority of instances the rises and falls in the Fed Index predate movements in the bond market. This relationship, of course, was the reason we had to calculate a lag in our implementation of the Fed Index into our portfolio management and also a reason for our trading model's steady performance.

* * *

Drawing numerous threads of esoteric market data into their estimations, while simultaneously affecting markets they appraise, the central bank presents Fed watchers with loaded words. Distilled into a single signal, these communications become an easily digestible, eminently actionable, and undoubtedly valuable data stream, arming financial professionals with vital information on the fixed-income markets. The Fed Index is that signal. Even taken as the lone trade signal, absent complex trading models or standard risk-reducing metrics, the Fed Index served as an extremely reliable portfolio manager, more than doubling the initial investment in a backtest that traversed the financial crisis. Portrayed graphically, this level of success is not too surprising. The Fed Index has a consistent, predictive correlation with the bond market, thereby serving as leading indicator of market fluctuations.

With the value of interpreting Fed communications as they relate to the fixed-income markets established, the next chapter moves to explore the increasingly powerful—but less apparent—connections that have developed between central bank communications and the equity markets.

8

Equity Market Investing: Macro Matters

The connection between central bank policy and fixed-income markets is clear, but the Fed's actions and words also find traction outside of bonds and bills. Equity markets, just like fixed income, also react to Fed communications. As Marcel Fratzscher, the former head of policy analysis at the European Central Bank, and Michael Ehrmann, the head of economic and financial research at Bank of Canada, have asserted, "Central bank communication is a statistically and economically important driver of financial markets" (Ehrmann and Fratzscher 2007). Economists and financial professionals have observed the budding ties between central bank dispatches and the equity markets in recent years, and our work integrating textual analysis with market reaction sheds additional light on this trend. Diving into the world of equities, this chapter explains the fundamentals underpinning equity markets. After covering the essentials, it then highlights the deep connections that have developed between central banks and equity movements—and the reasons behind this growing relationship. Finally, this chapter investigates the application of our central banking data to this space, demonstrating how our methodology could provide deeper insight into the ebb and flow of the modern equity markets.

* * *

Before exploring the connections between the Fed and these markets, a review of equities might be helpful. Almost every investment—fixed income, equities, or currencies—is structured like a loan. While the structure largely stays the same, the terms of repayment are what differentiate investment types. For fixed income, the terms are fairly straightforward: an investor purchases the instrument and, at some later date, gets cash back per the details of the agreement. Currencies are also relatively simple: an investor provides money to a bank, asking them to hold on to it in a foreign currency until the investor decides to take their money back at the value of that particular currency. Equities, however, are a bit more complex: the investor gets a piece of collateral—a share in the company—in exchange for their money, but the company is not ever explicitly required to pay the investor back unless a certain set of events occur. This commonly happens when a company is liquidated by sale or default. A shareholder is often entitled to a disbursement from the company as well (at the company's discretion), in proportion to the number of shares held. These practices hold true in nearly all cases for companies, private or public. Equity, as an asset class, is defined by receiving a stake in a company for your transaction.

Equity markets, by extension, are markets where shares of companies are bought and sold. In particular, the companies are publicly held; that is, shares of the company can be bought and sold by members of the general public. There are many exceptions to this, but the general rule is that shares of publicly held companies can be bought and sold on the open market. Typically, this occurs in an exchange—for instance, the New York Stock Exchange—which serves to simplify the transactions.

As with bonds, investors can purchase shares directly from companies. However, it is nearly always the case that companies only make their stock available through an exchange. Compared to bonds, there is essentially no distinction between primary and secondary markets. Additionally, companies typically only make a set number of shares available for purchase and, in most cases, an investor purchasing shares on the open market does so from a private individual or firm, not the company itself.

The buying and selling of equities is governed by bidding. Buyers list a bid price they are willing to pay for a share. Sellers offer up an ask price, the amount they are willing to accept for an offer. The gap between the two is referred to as the bid-ask spread. Prior to the digitization of the financial industry, traders on the exchange floor explicitly matched up buyers and sellers with matching bid and ask prices. Remember the scenes from movies where traders are shouting for attention? They are literally shouting prices and trying to find another trader with a potential customer at a particular price. The computerization of the process is a digital translation of this activity. The only major change is that there is now an explicit queuing mechanism as well, in which bids and asks are processed in the order they come into the system. Traders still do act on the floor, however, when unusual requests come in. The vast majority, however, is done electronically—a trend that translates to a quieter trading floor.

The price of equities is determined by market action, and market action is the conflation of an enormous collection of actors. There are, however, major players—players with huge wallets, vast portfolios, and influential voices. These are also powerful players who sway the equity markets, even if they do not often invest directly in them. And who are they? Central banks, of course.

* * *

The central bank tracks macroeconomic indicators to capture the state of current and potential future growth, and it adjusts policy accordingly. In most cases, the central bank is the single most informed expert on the health of the economy. As such, when it speaks of the health of the economy, its comments can reveal relatively unknown information. Reacting to this take on the state of the economy, investors make trading decisions, and scholars—along with the central banks themselves—have become increasingly interested in this connection. Referencing the conclusions of Fratzscher and Ehrmann, a recent paper by the Bank of Canada notes the impact of the Fed's word on equities: "The empirical results [...] also confirm that financial stability communications have a significant impact on asset prices [...] Equity markets move in line with the views in FSRs, and market volatility diminishes" (Vayid 2013, 16). Just a single communication from the Fed indicating contractionary monetary policy, as Ehrmann and Fratzscher have observed, was impactful enough to affect the US, UK, and eurozone equity markets (Ehrmann and Fratzscher 2007). And this relationship, especially since the financial crisis, has only deepened.

The reasons for this heightened connection are numerous. To begin with, the nature of central bank investment and its role in the market has dramatically evolved. In an attempt to support a struggling system, the Fed expanded its interests beyond treasuries, their traditional domain, and became a serious player in other asset markets. The Fed has pumped 4.5 trillion dollars into the economy over the last few years, and when such an enormous injection of liquidity floods into the economy, it will inevitably inflate asset values. These new moves by the central bank mean that the Fed also has more sway over the equity markets, making it highly improbable that any new policy will not have been rigorously evaluated in light of its impact on those markets. Beyond increasing their stake in the economy at large, their investments also give them another substantial form of leverage which they could use to powerfully influence the fortunes of other financial institutions with a vested interest in equity markets.

In addition to these new factors, the leadership shown by the central bank during the financial crisis has also bolstered the Fed's influence in this sphere—and the market as a whole. Even though more than half a decade has passed since the peak of the crisis, the confidence investors have in the entire system still depends largely on the actions the central bank takes. This dependency is, at least in part, the product of a market that has yet to fully regain its footing.

Another growing connection between Fed communication and the equity market lies in industry valuation methodology. It has now become standard practice for major financial institutions to take the central banks' moves into account when generating asset assessments. The "Fed model," which integrates data on the Federal Reserve's interest rate into equity evaluations, is a common tool for institutions like J. P. Morgan, ING, and Prudential—among others. As financial journalist Theo Casey wrote in 2010, "The fact is, influential market players embrace the Fed model [...] The net result is that the Fed model is a significant valuation tool which prominent investors use to check whether they should be buying stocks or bonds" (Casey 2010). Given this trend, it only makes more sense for equity market players to take a closer look at Fed dispatches: central bank communications foreshadow interest rates, which eventually bleed into equity attractiveness. Getting a good grasp of Fed communication puts them further up the chain of causality, allowing them to better anticipate future market conditions.

Taken together, these developments have afforded the Fed an unprecedented position, suggesting that financial professionals ought to pay closer attention to what an emerging market heavyweight has to say. As the Bank of Canada's Ianthi Vayid concluded in *Central Bank Communications Before, During and After the Crisis: From Open-Market Operations to Open-Mouth Policy*, "The fact remains that central bank talk on financial issues has attracted broad attention in the recent past and will be watched even more closely following the global crisis" (Vayid 2013, 17).

* * *

The Federal Reserve is, however, far from the only central bank that influences the equity markets. While it is rare that central banks directly invest in the equity markets, they are regularly affiliated with sovereign wealth and/or pension funds that are heavily invested in both fixed income and equity market assets. It is a well-known fact that sovereign wealth and public pension funds around the world have become large holders of company shares. One of the best-known examples is the Norwegian sovereign fund, Norges Bank Investment Management, with 880 billion dollars under management, of which more than 60 percent is invested in equities. The fund owns on average 1.3 percent of every globally listed company—and 2.5 percent of listed companies in Europe. As the biggest overall public-sector investor, the People's Bank of China (PBoC) wields tremendous influence over the equity market. The State Administration of Foreign Exchange, a division of the PBoC, has an astounding 3.9 trillion dollars under management, with investments that include significant holdings in Europe. (Recently, it appears that the PBoC itself has been directly buying minority equity stakes in important European companies; Marsh 2014.) The Bank of Japan (BOJ) and Japan's Government

Pension Investment Fund also represent substantial—although indirect—players in the equity markets, each with 1.3 trillion dollars invested. A major reason Japan's stock market has not collapsed (despite 20 years of flat economic growth) has been the resilience of its bond market (despite negative yields)—a market largely upheld by the constant influx of capital from Japanese institutional investors led by the BOJ. Another large public-sector equity owner is Swiss National Bank, ranked the world's No. 10 on the Global Progress Indicator by market assets, with 480 billion under management (Marsh 2014). Stateside, Calpers and Calsters represent the largest public pension funds in the nation and invest heavily in fixed-income and US equity markets. These are just a handful of the available examples—all of which point to the same conclusion: central banks around the world, and public funds associated with them, have tremendous sway in markets across asset classes, even equity markets. So, it should come as no surprise that what central bankers say is of vital importance to anyone operating in those spaces.

* * *

In light of these developments, understanding central bank communications has never been more important for market actors—a trend that translates directly into the relevance of our methodology.

As Figure 8.1 demonstrates, the Fed Index strongly correlates with the equity markets—in excess of 0.7 on a −1 to +1 scale. This means that more than 70 percent of the time equity markets are moving in lock step with our Federal Reserve sentiment data. As might be expected from the Fed's increasing influence and its simultaneous to unprecedented levels of transparency, the correlation between the Fed Index and the equity markets has been especially strong since the onset of the financial crisis. Of particular interest to investors, our Fed sentiment data is a consistent leading indicator with large Fed Index declines predating major market sell-offs, and thus, the data serves as a strong sell (or short) signal. In fact, the raw trend data demonstrates that the Fed Index was a consistent leading indicator for stock prices in the financial crisis.

To give a more detailed picture of the Fed Index's correlation with equity markets, the correlation graphs in Figures 8.2 and 8.3

EQUITY MARKET INVESTING   85

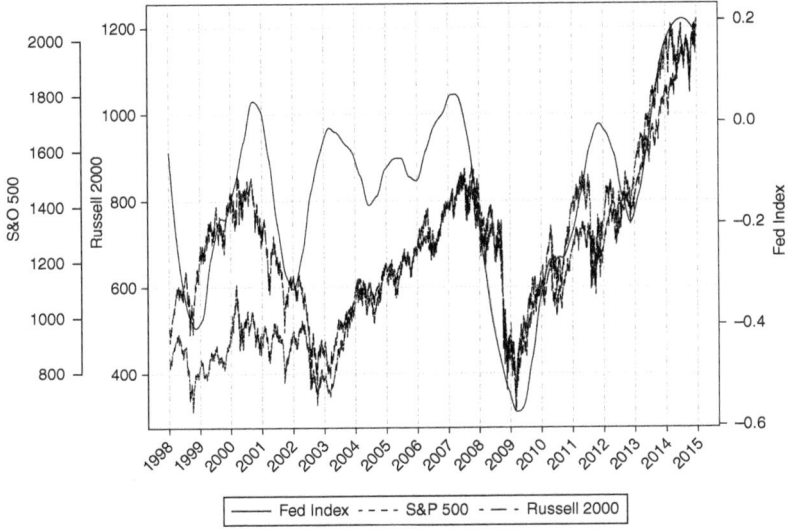

Figure 8.1   Fed Index, Russell 2K, S&P 500, and NASDAQ from 1997 to 2014.

break down the level of correlation within market indexes and individual equities.

These correlation graphs break down the markets into indexes and individual equities. In Figure 8.2, each individual bar represents a different index. In Figure 8.3, each individual bar represents a different equity. The strength of the correlation between our data and each of the indexes and equities is demonstrated in Figure 8.2 and 8.3 by the length of each bar. The possible correlation scores run from zero to 100—with 100 being perfect correlation and zero being no correlation. The data used to create these graphs spans 2007 to 2014.

The high level of correlation seen across the market and the extremely high correlations found in certain sectors and indexes reveal that the Fed Index is not only a good measure for looking at the market as a whole, but it also could prove useful for targeted analysis and developing sophisticated investment strategies. For example, Apple, Inc. (in the bottom third of Figure 8.3) shares over a 70 percent correlation to our sentiment data over the sample period. This means Apple moved in lockstep with the Fed more than 70 percent of the time from 2007 to 2014, despite numerous product releases, lawsuits, and other developments. This suggests that for investors interested

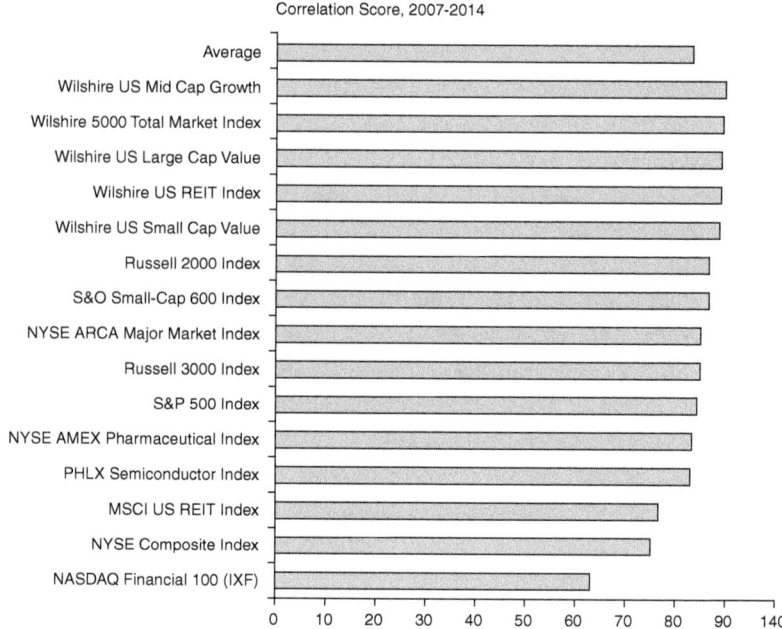

Figure 8.2 Correlation of Fed Index with standard market indexes.

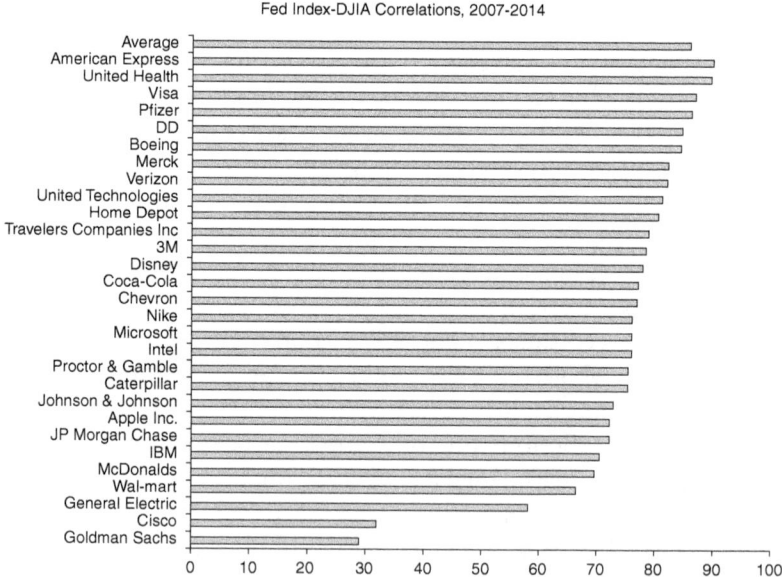

Figure 8.3 Correlation of Fed Index with industrial sector indexes.

in Apple stock, the Fed Index represents a powerful means of understanding that investment. Such targeted analysis is made even more effective by the speed at which the data is available: the Fed Index can be generated in real time (typically less than ten seconds after the issuance of a communication). Fast, high-quality signals are exactly what traders need to make the best decisions possible, and, with detailed, actionable data available in real time, the Fed Index represents the cutting edge in investor information.

* * *

As we did with fixed income, we also backtested the Fed Index as the manager of an equity portfolio. Using a 100 percent equity portfolio with standard sector weightings and no leverage, we ran a long-only simulation from 2007 to 2014. The portfolio yielded 70 percent returns, beating major market indexes by over 30 percent, and Figure 8.4 illustrates its performance.

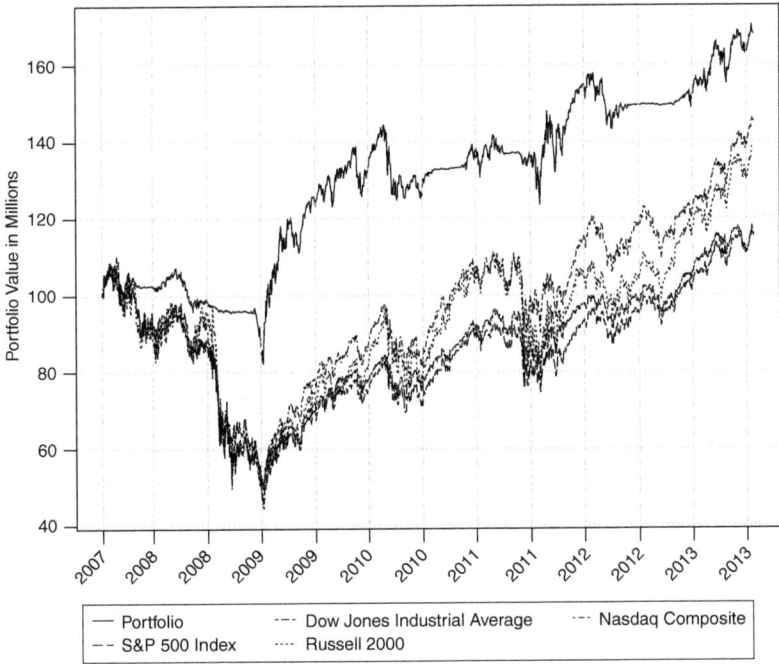

Figure 8.4 Fed Index-driven simulated stock portfolio value, compared to major indexes.

As with the fixed-income backtest, our portfolio sidestepped the market crash by serving as a vital sell indicator and highlighting the Fed Index usefulness as a wealth preservation tool. Our portfolio never went down more than 18 percent—even when equity indexes suffered losses greater than 50 percent. Leveraging recent developments in the Fed's economic role, the Fed Index is not only insightful financial data—but could be put to work as high-level decision maker as well.

* * *

Traditionally, equity analysts left Fed watching to the fixed-income folks, but recent years have seen a consistent impact of the Fed's dispatches on equity markets. This means that for those interested in understanding the flow of these markets, central bank communications have become essential data. By rapidly aggregating and objectively interpreting central bank texts in real time, the Fed Index allows market players to get a detailed picture of the central bank's influence on equity markets. The next chapter will expand on the utility of the Fed Index, elaborating on its performance as a forecasting tool.

9

Forecasting Policy: Market Response to Fed Communication Trends

Is it possible to foresee the future of the financial market? Initial analysis does not offer much hope. The thought of the nearly infinite factors at play in any market fluctuation would seem to immediately stifle even the most sophisticated techniques. But, regardless of how overwhelming prediction may be, it is a necessary precondition to action—financial or otherwise. Every investment decision financial professionals make is predicated on a projection, impossible as it may be, of what economic developments lie ahead. So the question is not really whether or not it is possible, in a strict sense, to predict the future of the financial markets. Its possibility is secondary to its necessity. The question is, instead, "what is the best way to tackle the impossible?"

In finance, the business of tackling the impossible is known as forecasting, and this chapter tackles this topic head on. Beginning with a discussion of what forecasting is, the following pages discuss how an accurate assessment of the Federal Reserve's attitude—in a world where its voice is an increasingly powerful market driver—might serve as an incredibly valuable forecasting tool.

* * *

Forecasting is an extension of a theory or trend into the future. The foundation of any (credible) forecast is an extensive set of observations—a wide breadth of data about whatever circumstance is under investigation. In finance, that data set could include prices, interest rates, fixed-income and equity market trends, gross domestic product estimates, capital-asset ratios, etc. These observations, naturally, lead to a hypothesis—an educated model of how something works. The historical data that was the source of the hypothesis at once becomes its best means of assessment. In other words, the efficacy of any model can easily be measured against the test of history: given a restricted data set—observations all made before a specific date—can that model predict what will happen next? Naturally, the most successful models are those that are best able to project the "future" outcomes of historical circumstances.

These models are not meant to reflect the full complexity of the processes and systems upon which they are based. Instead, the best models are an efficient distillation of these mechanics, bringing accessibility to the real-life processes that are otherwise too dense and unwieldy to understand. In finance, the necessity of modeling is obvious. The financial markets produce a deluge of data, and it quickly becomes incredibly difficult to differentiate useful signal from useless noise. Strong models capture the movement of the essential gears of the system, presenting an intelligible picture of the present and, even more powerfully, a handle on the future. That is a forecast.

* * *

The advantages of effective forecasting tools are numerous. In finance, these advantages all orbit the same concept: maximizing resources. Perhaps the most immediately apparent of these advantages is the ability to leverage opportunities and avoid dangers that others do not—or cannot—see. If an investor can get a sense of the future landscape, this prescient perspective would allow that investor to allocate resources to create the best possible return. While boosting gains, effective forecasting also serves as a valuable risk management tool, helping investors minimize the inevitable losses that attend any sustained market activity. In the ever-increasing opacity of the modern financial system, losses can occur for any number of reasons—not the least among these being poor forecasting. A recent article in the *New York Times* recounted the high cost of erroneous predictions:

> In October, the World Bank estimated that the costs associated with Ebola for West Africa as a whole may be as high as $32.6 billion, an estimate that was revised down this month to be at most $6 billion. When the public anticipates bad times, they cut back on discretionary purchases and save more, compounding the effects of the shock [...] collectively focusing on worst-case scenarios can make people fatalistic, damaging efforts to prevent the disease from spreading. It also has a negative effect on the economy and makes it harder for those seeking to raise money for future crises. Independent data sources and assessments are vital to our understanding of and response to the crisis. (Glennerster, M'cleod, and Suri 2015)

While projections are a necessary for any endeavor, not all forecasts are created equal. Preparing for the worst-case scenario can seem like a safe bet, but it actually can—as in the case of the Ebola outbreak—cause an even greater problem than would have otherwise developed. Quality forecasting can minimize the costs associated with overestimating future challenges, allowing any sort of plan—investment plans certainly included—to appropriately skirt the dividing line between caution and risk.

Effective forecasting methods further compound their efficiency by being able to generate accurate predictions with less data than other models might require. Gathering data can be an expensive proposition—research does not come cheap—and the best forecasting tools are able cut down on these costs by operating more efficiently.

All these advantages translate into a strong platform for confident, successful leadership. The better the grasp any leader has on what could happen, the more assured they can be that the decision made was the best possible, allowing them to more convincingly impart their vision to those around them. In the financial world, this confidence could manifest itself in any number of ways. For executives, it could increase their effectiveness communicating the company's stability to their employees. For wealth managers, it could bolster their confidence during client-facing meetings. In any case, sound projections arm their receivers with the kind of data-backed assurance that financial professionals need to take the lead when facing the unknown.

* * *

The Fed is certainly accustomed to attempts at forecasting their policy—however questionable these forecasting methodologies have been. The briefcase watch was an early attempt at predicting the central bank's next steps. The modern practice of Fed watching is inundated with forecasting attempts. Analysts scrutinize meeting minutes and press releases to build a case for a certain policy projection (stating, for example, that in six months the Fed will begin to increase interest rates) and this practice can, at times, produce accurate predictions.

Built on a foundation of historical market reaction to Fed communications, our methodology is also capable of producing predictions. This foundation is part of what distinguishes our forecasting from the rest of an already large industry actively engaged in monetary policy speculation. Our predictions are generated within the framework of the Fed Index, allowing us to produce complete statistical forecasting of future monetary policy and, based on established correlations to various assets, forecasts of asset prices.

Inside the Federal Reserve, monetary policy emerges from collaborative effort. Multiple actors submit information relevant to decisions, and the Federal Open Market Committee (FOMC) meets as a group to consider future monetary policy. When central bankers communicate, their speeches and press releases emerge out of this collaboration and reveal a very particular set of data: the information they used to set current policy and, based on what they saw before, how they expect their policy to change. Since there appears to be a regular relationship between past and current information, we can use statistical tools to bridge that gap, and make predictions about their future position. In essence, our process not only allows us to understand the relationship between the words the Fed chooses and the market, but also the relationship these words have to each other. From here, we are now able to map what a central bank has done in the past onto what they are doing in the present and, most importantly, with what they will do in the future.

Our forecasts are made, in short, by generating a future sentiment analytic from the previous sentiment scores.

* * *

The Fed Index data has allowed us to consistently and accurately predict the sentiment of upcoming FOMC meetings. Figure 9.1 represents a backtesting run assessing precisely that ability—forecasting FMOC scores—and the results confirmed our methodology.

Each of the dots in Figure 9.1 are the actual FOMC meeting scores and the lines intersecting the dots are our projections. The difference in the line width is representative of our level of confidence. The thicker portions of each line indicate that we have 80 percent confidence that the coming score will fall within that space; the thinner portions indicate that we are 95 percent sure that the future meetings mood will be captured in that line. Each prediction is made a week before the meeting, utilizing only what information would have been available to us at that time. Most of the dots are

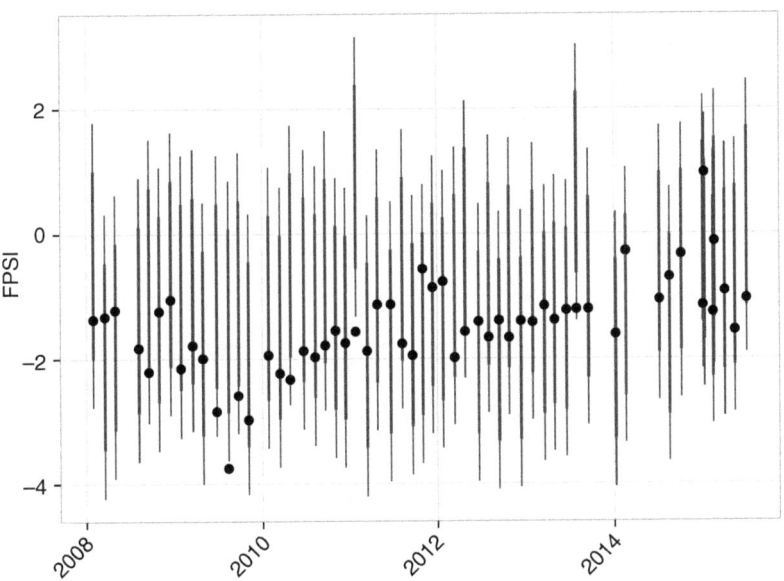

Figure 9.1 FOMC meetings forecast, one-week lag.

in the middle of our prediction range, indicating that our forecasts consistently anticipate the correct values of upcoming meeting. Even in the rare cases (2 out of 53) where the actual meeting scores fall outside our forecasted values, they—without exception—fall back inside our projections by the next meeting. As the results—covering an almost eight-year period—attest, our forecasts can be called upon as reliable predictors of the Fed's mood.

* * *

But, beyond efficiently projecting the central bank attitude, the Fed Index also allows us to forecast complex, even seemingly unexpected, policy decisions. In September of 2013 the market expectation was that the Federal Reserve would begin "tapering" asset purchases (see Figure 9.2 for details).

The Fed Index indicated sentiment was rising at that time, and this rise indicates a trend toward a more hawkish position. The tapering of asset purchases is a hawkish policy by the central bank because it curbs capital injection into the economy, thereby cooling the economic engine. But, within the context of recent historical data, it was obvious that the Fed would not begin tapering

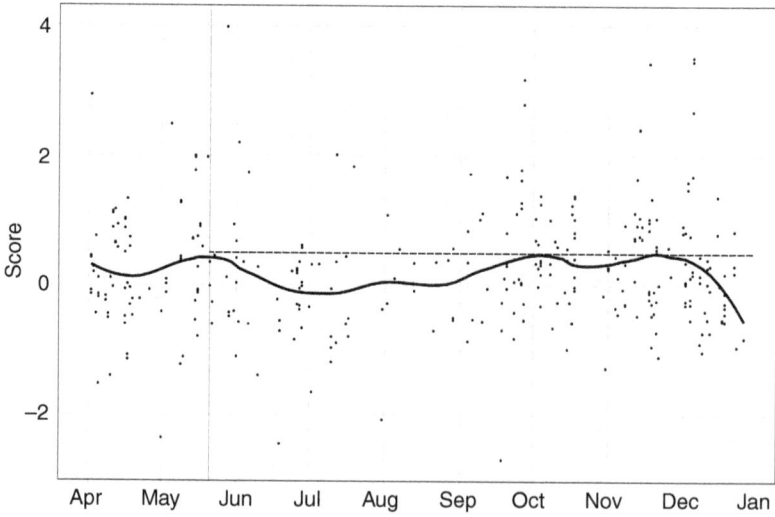

Figure 9.2 Fed Index six-month moving average, April–September 2013.

yet. The six-month Fed Index trend demonstrates that although sentiment was rising in September, it remained below highs from April and May. Even during those months tapering was still seen as unlikely, and because the current score—while rising—remained below those highs, we projected that it was unlikely the Fed would begin tapering. While contradicting popular market opinion, our policy predictions were validated: the Fed did not begin tapering in September; they waited until December of 2013 to initiate tapering.

In reference to the December 2013 tapering meeting, our forecast of that meeting's score serves as yet another example of the reliability of our forecasting methodology. Four days ahead of the meeting, we correctly predicted (trend line) the sentiment of the FOMC meeting (indicated on graph) (see Figure 9.3 for details).

The near-perfect correlation between the forecasted score and the actual score exemplifies the high level of forecasting accuracy our methodology can generate—an accuracy made all the more impressive by the limited data required to generate it. As was discussed above, an essential aspect of a powerful forecasting technique

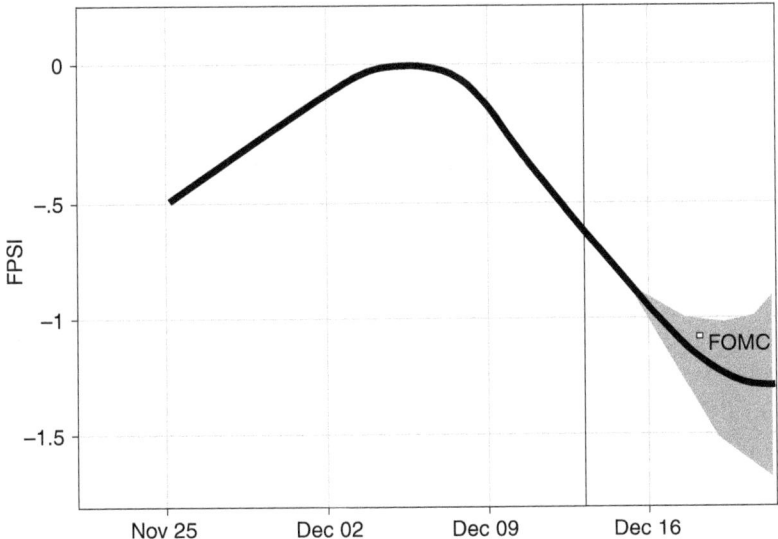

Figure 9.3 Fed Index projection as of December 14, 2013, and actual FOMC sentiment.

is efficiency (cost effectiveness), and our projections, which emerge purely from our analysis of central banking texts and the market, represent a powerful marriage of thrift and accuracy.

The accuracy of our forecast—and inaccuracy of mainstream projections—reinforces a particular strength of our process—and, conversely, a particular weakness of others. As has been discussed in earlier chapters, human analysis consistently falls prey to human errors, one of which is an unjustified prejudice toward recent events and trends. It seems understandable, given the central bank's trend toward hawkish communications in August and September, that analysts might have predicted tapering. Those predictions, it seems, were the product of a recency bias—and possibly groupthink as well. It is not uncommon, after all, for an initial prediction to gain undue credibility from bandwagon support. When the larger, more objective picture comes into focus, a picture that the Fed Index is the product of, the true improbability of that forecast becomes apparent. The central bank is a creature of habit and history, and, as such, its policy moves should be predicted using processes that take that full context into account.

* * *

Even without using past values of the Fed Index to project future values of the signal—and therefore future market reactions—the signal can be used as a forecasting tool. This is possible because central bank communications (or more accurately, our proprietary interpretations of them) have a fundamentally predictive relationship with the market. Fed communications are digested by the financial markets at varying speeds and the individual markets each react in different ways, but, in any case, it takes time—ranging from nanoseconds to years—for the Fed's words to act on the economy. Therefore, if current communications can be evaluated in light of historical market reactions, the interpretation produced is not just a snapshot of what is—it is a vision of what's to come. As is the case with every portfolio in every market we've backtested, a lag has to be engineered into the process precisely because of this fact: our central bank sentiment data is, inherently, a projection of the future economic landscape, making virtually every signal we produce a leading indicator (from which a forecast can also be generated).

And this projection can yield significant foresight. For instance, in the fixed-income backtesting covered in an earlier chapter we discovered that the market took 193 days to align with the Fed's sentiment. This means that the Fed Index generated a six-month leading indicator on the fixed-income market—a full two-quarters in advance.

This projection can also yield significant alpha (returns in excess of benchmark). Even without sophisticated forecasting based on correlations to particular assets, the Fed Index is an incredibly effective portfolio management tool when simply used as a leading indicator. We ran tests using the Fed Index as a four-week leading indicator and the only buy/sell signal with a sample long-only portfolio holding 80 percent equities, 20 percent fixed income with standard sector weightings, and no leverage. Running from 2007 to 2014, our sample portfolio yielded a 50 percent return, outperforming major market indexes by roughly 30 percent. The results are presented in Figure 9.4.

Closer analysis only makes the portfolio's performance more notable. While markets plummeted during the throes of the

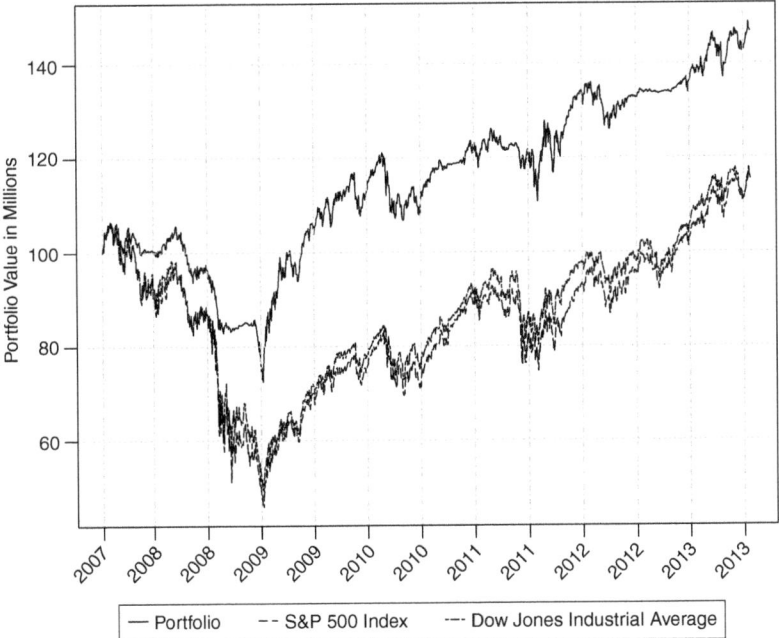

Figure 9.4 Fed Index-led portfolio, the S&P 500, and the Dow Jones.

financial crisis, with benchmarks like the S&P 500 and the Dow Jones Industrial suffering losses in excess of 50 percent, our long-only Fed Index-driven portfolio declined, at the very worst, by only 12 percent. For financial professionals, the Fed Index's prescient relationship with the market could become an effective means of mitigating downside risk—or even capitalizing on it via a long-short strategy.

* * *

Forecasting is a tricky business. There are numerous signals from which to divine information, vast amounts of historical data to sort through, and endless competing models to evaluate based on various combinations of all this information. Taken all at once, the tools and data available can seem as daunting to process as the unknown that each forecasting method seeks to demystify. Given all the noise and clutter, it makes sense to boil down an overwhelming process to its essentials, and, for financial professionals, those essentials are fundamental market movers. The Fed is the preeminent market mover, and its central role in the modern financial landscape means that a good grasp of the central bank's processes can enable a rational and effective forecast of the future of the entire economy. Using a detailed and comprehensive history of the central bank, the Fed Index allows for such predictions and, as statistical testing has validated, those predictions are remarkably accurate. For investors, traders, financial advisors, portfolio managers—or anyone interested in finance—these forecasts represent a powerful tool for strengthening their handle on the future of financial markets.

10

FOREX Investing: Central Bank Sentiment Data across the Globe

With command over the Treasury's dollar production (which are called Federal Reserve Notes) and interest rates, the Fed directly influences both the quantity and price of money more than any other actor. Given its central role in upholding the integrity of the currency, it makes sense to regard the central bank's words not only as authoritative assessments of the state of the dollar, but also as catalysts for market movement themselves. As sensible as this deduction seems, it is surprising to note how little this connection has been researched. Although numerous scholars—especially since the financial crisis—have evaluated the role of central bank communications in the financial markets and the effect of those communications on currencies, money itself, as noted German economist Marcel Fratzscher explains, has yet to be widely explored:

> While there is broad agreement that actual [foreign exchange] purchases or sales may affect exchange rates under certain conditions [...], hardly any work has been done on the issue of whether oral interventions may be effective, apart from [Jansen and de Haan's work] and [Fratzscher's work]. (Fratzscher 2008, 1652)

For financial professionals, the better handle they have on the relationship between central bank dispatches and money, the better their understanding of the FOREX market. Our work analyzing the relationship between central bank communications and the financial markets has ideally positioned us to assess this relationship. This chapter begins with an in-depth discussion of the impact central bank policy has on money, and, then, leveraging the insight afforded by our sentiment analysis data, it explores the significant role central banking dispatches play in FOREX.

* * *

With a suite of monetary levers at hand, the Fed is obviously a central figure when it comes to money—but the details of the interplay between institution and currency are harder to appraise than might be expected. This analysis does not get any easier when the entire FOREX market is examined. The sheer number and variety of players who have a hand in determining the value of one currency vis-à-vis another can make the task of assessing the full measure and nature of the Fed's hand in this sphere a daunting task, but, details aside, there is no denying the intervening hand of the central bank:

> We find contemporaneous positive correlation between the direction of intervention and the conditional mean and variance of exchange rate returns. We show that sustained and large interventions have a stabilising influence in the foreign exchange market in terms of direction and volatility. Without these interventions, the market would have moved further and exhibited more volatility. (Kim and Sheen 2002)

University of Michigan Economics Professor Katherine Dominguez has also noted the power of the central banks on FOREX, finding that between 1977 and 1994 interventions by the Fed were responsible for more than 40 percent of the exchange rate volatility between the US dollar and the Japanese yen (Dominguez 1998). The fact that the Fed contributes to the volatility of the currency should not be confused with lack of control: the central bank may increase the change in value to achieve a desired outcome—often steadying the currency in the long run. Instead, what the Fed's contribution to volatility does communicate is the impact the Fed has on the currency market.

Recently, the power central banks have over this market has been a hot topic in the mainstream financial media, as the brewing "currency wars" are, according to the *Wall Street Journal*, "driven by central banks":

> Half the central banks representing the Group of 20 developed and large emerging economies, whose top monetary and finance officials meet to discuss the global economy this week in Istanbul, have taken easing steps so far this year. The moves—mainly in the form of interest-rate cuts but also asset purchases—have ricocheted through foreign-exchange markets, driving the currencies of some countries down and those of others, primarily the U.S., up. (Blackstone 2015)

As central banks continue to play their integral role as the guardians of currency, their voices represent critical market information—informing and influencing the tide of currencies around the globe.

* * *

How influential are central banking communications on exchange rates? Marcel Fratzscher calculates that in G3 (United States, Europe, and Japan) economies, the "effects of oral interventions are, on average, around 0.15–0.20% on the level of the US dollar—euro and yen—US dollar exchange rates" (Fratzscher 2008, 1671). While the numbers may seem small, it is important to correctly place these percentages in context. When taking into account that the FOREX market sees daily trading volume in the trillions of dollars, fluctuations in the tenths of a percent means could mean billion dollar shifts. As Fratzscher notes, communications seem particularly influential when they run contrary to the rest of policy:

> As an order of magnitude, for the US an oral intervention against the mantra has the same effect on the US dollar exchange rate as a USD 1.2 billion actual intervention against the euro and USD 1.9 billion actual intervention against the yen. Overall, the results emphasize the remarkable effectiveness of oral interventions if they occur against the prevalent policy stance. Finally, actual interventions have mostly increased the conditional variances of the exchange rates on the days following interventions. By contrast, oral interventions have in most cases decreased the volatility. (Fratzscher 2008, 1671)

Not only can "oral interventions" (guiding central banking communications known as forward guidance in the United States) have the same impact on the market as billions of dollars, but the effect words have (as opposed to enacted policy) seem preferable—soothing volatility. Wielding this level of power, communications have become an ascendant tool of policy for central banks looking to make their mark on FOREX:

> Exchange rate policies in many economies have undergone a fundamental regime change since the mid-1990s. Monetary authorities in the United States and the euro area have basically abandoned actual interventions in 1995 and have shifted towards the use of communication, or oral interventions, to convey their stance on exchange rates to the markets. (Fratzscher 2008, 1651)

This trend not only makes understanding central bank communications important for analyzing the FOREX market, it actually makes these speeches required reading. But, as Fratzscher (2008) has observed, the details of the relationship remain relatively untouched by economic research, which, for those with a vested interest in understanding the market, is an unfortunate coincidence.

* * *

In order to get a clearer look at the connections between communications and exchange rates, at least two following data streams are needed:

1. A history of FOREX rates.
2. A history of central banking communications in terms of market reactions.

The first of these is readily available, and the second could be supplied by our methodology. Ideally, the data on central banking texts should extend beyond one side of a currency pair. In other words, the Fed Index may help unlock the connection between the Fed's language and the dollar, but, when it comes to FOREX, it is obvious that the connection between other central banks' communications and their respective currencies would have enormous bearing on the final relationship among the multitude of currencies interacting in this market. Fortunately, the Fed Index is not the only data set our process has allowed us to generate. Using the same market-reaction-to-communication relationship that allowed us to produce the Fed Index, we have been able to create historical and real-time sentiment data streams on nearly every major central bank in the world.

With this information in hand, the connections that exist between these institutions and the FOREX market become easier to spot.

* * *

For a fuller picture of these dynamics, the next few pages dive into a more detailed, particular analysis by walking through different currency pairs as they interact with central bank communications.

USD, Basket of Currencies, and the Fed

In Figure 10.1, the solid black line is the Fed Index. The broken line is the exchange rate between the USD and a weighted average of

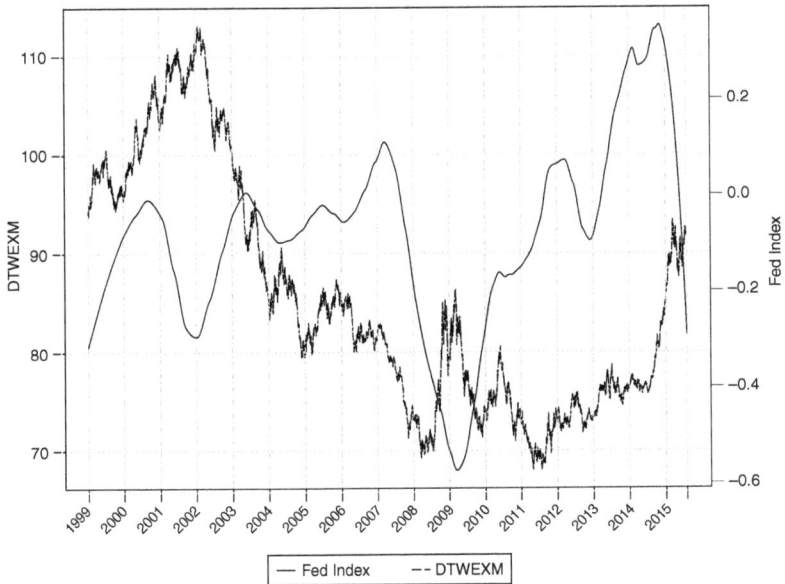

Figure 10.1 USD-basket of currencies with Fed Index.

major world currencies. As this line reaches higher or lower values, it indicates that the dollar is, respectively, reaching higher or lower values. From the early months of 2009 onward, the slow (albeit volatile) ascension of the solid line indicated that the Fed has become more hawkish—a trend that peaks in early 2014. As a hawkish central bank is looking to increase the value of their currency, the Fed's brooding hawkishness could be expected to later manifest in a climbing dollar. Interestingly, Figure 10.1 illustrates exactly that, as the value of USD gradually travels from approximately 70 units in the middle of 2008 to almost 95 units in early 2015.

USD, EUR, the Fed, and the ECB

In Figure 10.2, the broken and dotted line is the value of the euro in dollars; the broken line is the sentiment of the Fed, and the solid black line is the sentiment of the European Central Bank. As noted above, since the beginning of 2009, the Fed has trended toward hawkishness. The ECB's attitude in the same period, on the other hand, has orbited the same dovish values, oscillating from approximately 0.2 to negative 0.8. The Fed's hawkish communications would encourage a deflationary dollar—increasing its value;

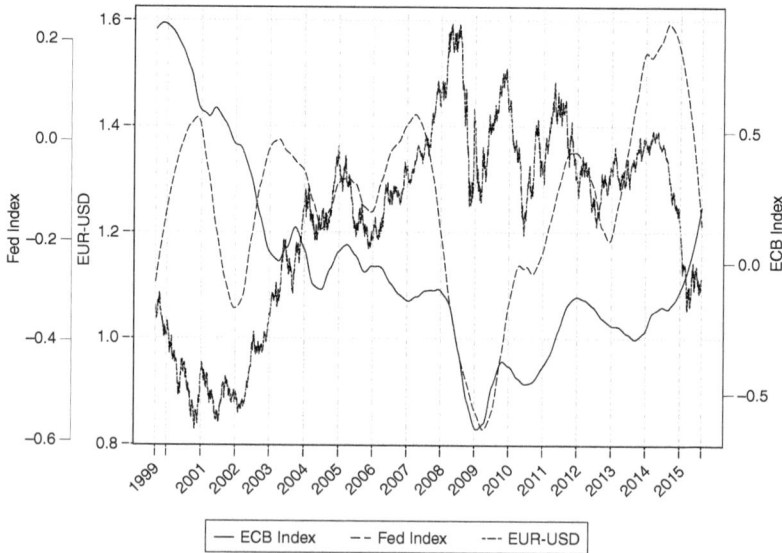

Figure 10.2 ECB-USD with bank trends.

conversely, the ECB's dovish dispatches would inspire the euro to inflation. Given the sentiment data, it might be predicted that the value of the euro relative to the dollar would begin to plummet, and, once again, when Figure 10.2 is consulted, that is exactly what is seen: as the Fed becomes more hawkish and the ECB remains dovish, the euro rapidly loses ground to the dollar. These attitudes, in turn, give the currency a higher value relative to the euro.

USD, GBP, the Fed, and the BOE

The pound (GBP) in dollars is represented in Figure 10.3 by the dotted and broken lines, and the solid black and broken lines are sentiments of the Bank of England (BOE) and the Fed, respectively. In general, since the financial crisis the Fed and the BOE seem to move in tandem toward an increasingly hawkish attitude, with the Fed's attitude showing the most dramatic fluctuations. The synchronization of the banks' sentiment might lead to the expectation that the value of the pound relative to the dollar would stay relatively steady, and Figure 10.3 largely bears out these expectations with the pound holding between 1.4 and 1.7 dollars since 2009.

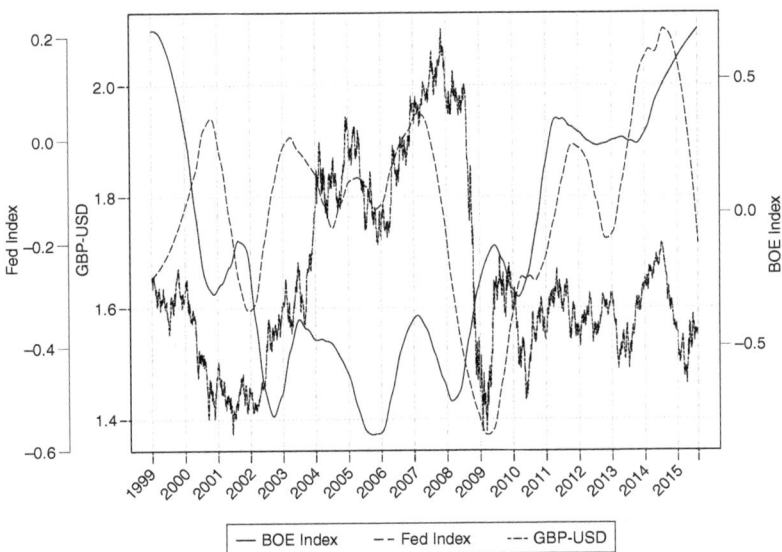

Figure 10.3 GBP-USD with bank trends.

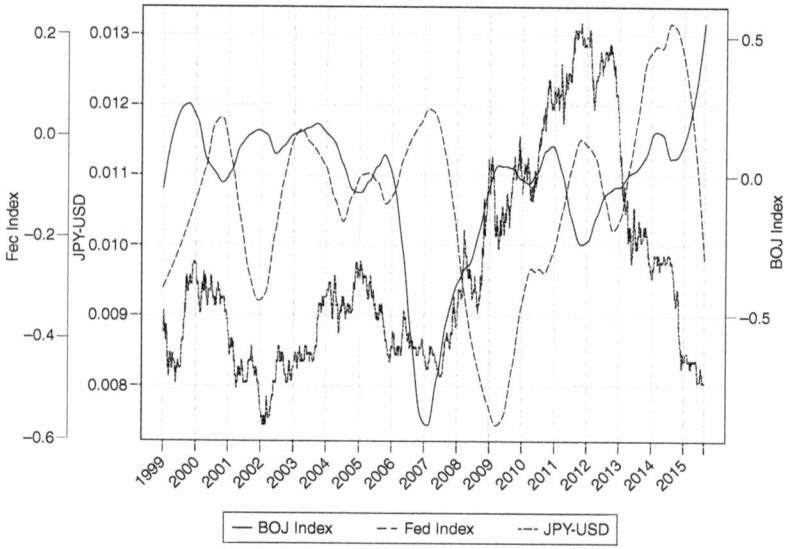

Figure 10.4 JPY-USD with bank trends.

USD, JPY, the Fed, and the BOJ

In Figure 10.4, the dotted and broken line represents the yen (JPY) in terms of the dollar. The mood of the Bank of Japan (BOJ) is reflected as the solid black line—the Fed's mood by the broken line. From 2008 to 2011, the BOJ and the Fed seem to have an inverse relationship: as the BOJ's hawkishness peaks, the Fed is in a dovishness dive and vice versa. This dynamic seems to have a direct bearing on the value of the yen relative to the dollar; during this period, for instance, every time the Fed becomes strongly dovish and the BOJ more hawkish, the dollar value of the yen begins to climb sharply. Before 2011, the Fed's hawkish highs are still lower than the BOJ's, and this difference seems related to the continual rise of the yen until the end of 2012, when the hawkishness of the Fed causes the dollar to jump in value and, simultaneously, the BOJ's massive monetary stimulus devalued the yen.

CAD, USD, the Fed, and the BOC

In Figure 10.5, the broken and dotted line indicates the value of the Canadian dollar (CAD)—also known as the loonie—in

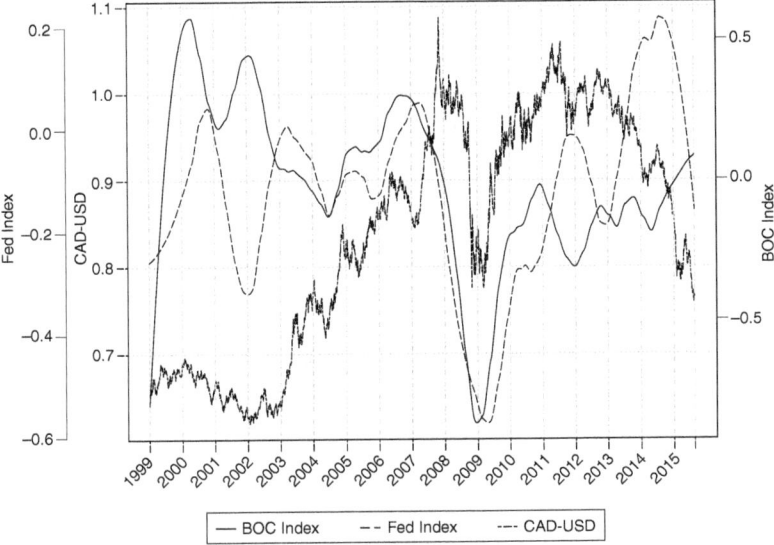

Figure 10.5 CAD-USD with bank trends.

terms of the US dollar; the solid black line is mood of the Bank of Canada, and the broken line is the mood of the Fed. From 2009 on, the sentiment of the two banks seems closely correlated—only significantly decoupling in the middle of 2014 when the Fed's hawkishness abruptly climbs and the BOC's drops. From this data, it could be projected that the value of the loonie relative to the dollar would generally steady from after the crisis until 2014, when its value should suddenly drop. This forecast is largely vindicated in Figure 10.5, where from the end of 2009 on the exchange rate hovers around 0.9 from 2010 until 2014, when value of the loonie begins to rapidly decline.

USD, CNY, AUD, the Fed, and the RBA

At first, the lumping of AUD, CNY, and USD together may seem like an odd combination, but there is method to the madness. Of the central banks we study, the PBoC is one of the most important (it oversees the second largest economy in the world)—and one of the most opaque (which is the reason that the sentiment of the PBoC is not reflected in Figures 10.6 and 10.7). And this opacity is

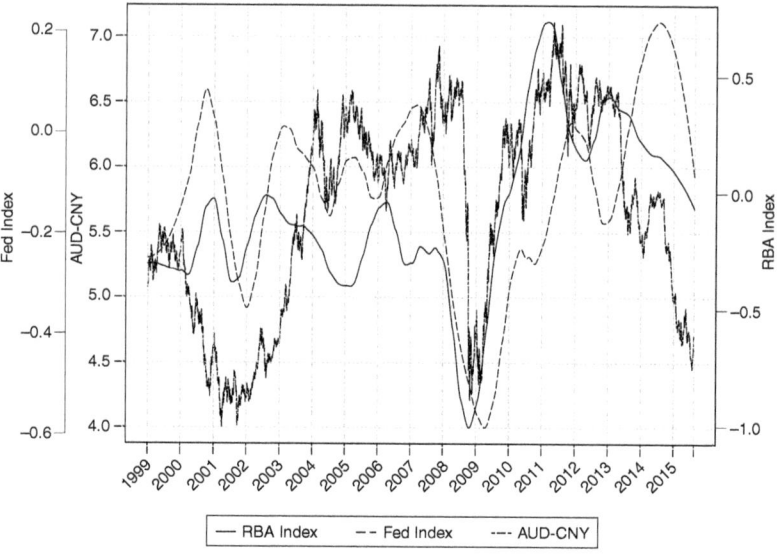

Figure 10.6 AUD-CNY with bank trends.

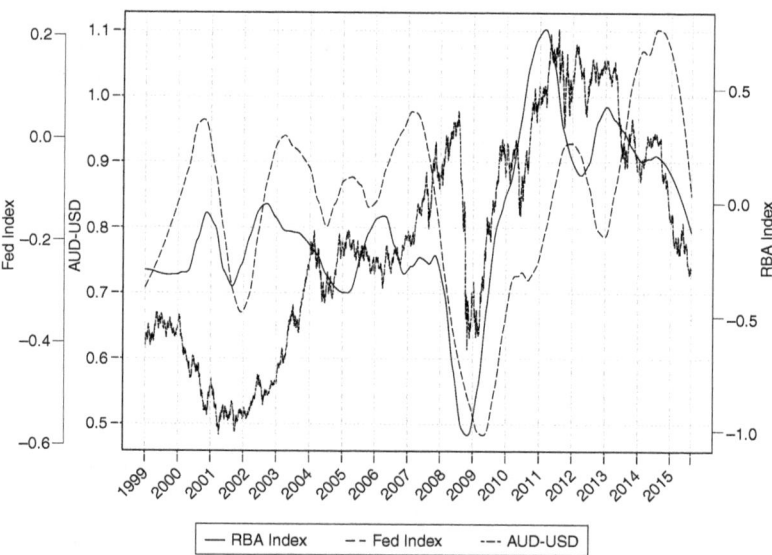

Figure 10.7 AUD-USD with bank trends.

also present in the official data regarding the Chinese economy as a whole. To work around this opacity, it becomes necessary to use other financial institutions as a proxy to understand the Chinese economy. This proxy, as might have been guessed, is the Reserve Bank of Australia (RBA). Over last couple of decades, RBA movements have been tied to China, and this relationship, as Bloomberg explains, is one born from dependency:

> Australia is the most China-dependent developed economy in the world, with exports to the nation accounting for 5.3 percent of gross domestic product, according to Commonwealth Bank of Australia, as two-way trade reached about A$150 billion ($132 billion) in 2013. Policy makers want to rebalance growth drivers from resources to other areas like services, which account for 70 percent of GDP but just 17 percent of exports. (Heath 2014)

As of 2015, Australia has secured a free trade agreement with China, so it can only be expected that this dynamic will continue (Heath 2014)—a dynamic captured in Figures 10.6 and 10.7.

In Figures 10.6 and 10.7, the Fed is represented by a broken line and the RBA by a solid black line. In Figure 10.6, the broken and dotted line is the Australian dollar (AUD) in terms of the Chinese yuan (CNY); in the second, the broken and dotted line is the Australian dollar in terms of the US dollar. Since the recession, the RBA has made a steady climb toward a more hawkish position through the beginning of 2013. Therefore, it would be expected that the currency would appreciate in value over the same period. Against both the USD and the CNY, the Australian dollar made significant gains during that time span—peaking at about 1.1 USD and 7 CNY per AUD in mid-2011 (immediately after the RBA's peak hawkish score of almost 1). But while it seems that the RBA has maintained its relatively hawkish mood to keep pace with the yuan, it appears that PBoC's disinflationary measures have been too rapid to catch. This development can be clearly seen from 2011 on, during which time the gap between the yuan and the AUD has dropped by a third (from 7 to 1 to almost 4.5 to 1). The sentiment and exchange rate trends portrayed in Figures 10.6 and 10.7 would seem to point to decelerating growth in the Chinese economy.

It is noteworthy that in both Figures 10.6 and 10.7, the correlation between the RBA's sentiment and the exchange rates (again, since the financial crisis) is high, and this is especially true in Figure 10.7. The AUD–USD seems to reflect RBA (and, by extension, the Chinese economy) very closely, with sentiment peaks and valleys mirrored in the exchange rates approximately a month later. This steady relationship could serve as a useful indicator for future fluctuations.

As a whole, these observations only represent the very beginning of what could be learned from closer examinations of central bank communications. As we—and others—continue to build more effective analytical tools and dive deeper into the patterns that emerge in the data we have already generated, the significance of the role of central banks will more fully come into view.

* * *

While it seems clear that better understanding of central bank sentiment affords FOREX players additional insight into market flows, the importance of this data extends beyond currency trade. For investors, currency dynamics play an important role throughout the financial landscape—including equity and fixed-income investments. Both equities and fixed income move in their native currencies; thus, foreign currency moves play directly into equity values. For example, if an equity is priced at 10 euros, and the dollar is roughly the same value as the euro, then that equity is worth approximately 10 dollars. But if the dollar appreciates relative to the euro, then the equity is now priced at 9 dollars—even though it is still worth 10 euros. This obviously translates to a tremendous opportunity for those looking to buy with dollars—an advantage that only increases as the scale of the transaction grows. Similarly, currency fluctuations should be taken into account when dealing with fixed income investments—especially when holding significant foreign debt. If China, for instance, holds 1 trillion dollars of US fixed income bonds purchased for 7 yuan per dollar and the yuan begins to appreciate relative to the dollar—5 yuan now equaling a dollar—China will have lost trillions of yuan. In other words, where a trade would have earned China 7 yuan per dollar, it now will earn 5 yuan, and that difference, multiplied by a trillion, would result in a loss of 2 trillion yuan. With both fixed income and equities, the more predictable currency fluctuations are for financial professionals, the better they will be able to navigate the complexities of relative value trades in international investing.

* * *

Processing almost unfathomable sums on a daily basis through countless split second transactions, the FOREX market stands as one of the most complicated and influential systems on the planet. As money is the means by which the value of goods and services is quantified, FOREX tremors carry consequences throughout the global economy. For many studying this space, any new insight into the gears of this vast machine is undeniably useful. As central banks continue to turn toward communications as a method of influencing exchange rates, the data we have begun to produce could not only give some additional insight into the market—especially considering the data we generate on both sides of many currency pairs—it could also provide a window into the biggest drivers of currency movements.

PART III

Global Monetary Policy: Analyzing Central Banks around the World

11

ECB Sentiment: Decoding a Complex Monetary Union

Transparency, and the implications it has for those who study the world of finance, is the central thread of this book. From the origin of the Fed to the financial crisis and beyond, the last two parts have tackled the development of this central banking strategy, discussing the attempts that others and we have made to interpret the wealth of text that now flows from the Federal Reserve. But, as has been discussed in early chapters, transparency is a trend that far exceeds American borders. Although the first experiments in central banking transparency were the product of the Volcker era, transparency began in earnest overseas, when, in the mid-1980s, the Bank of England began issuing press releases. In short, transparency has been an international movement for several decades. Part III of this book examines the state of this global phenomenon—an account that begins with Europe's leviathan, the European Central Bank (ECB).

But our account is not limited to the rise of open central banking policy around the world—the relevance of our work in textual analysis is an additional, essential storyline to this narrative. Just as transparency has been, in equal parts, a blessing and a challenge for Fed watchers, central bank analysts the world over are also grappling with a mounting cascade of market-moving information and the tremendous potential this data represents for the financial community. We believe that these data streams can afford more objective, quantifiable, and actionable information than they currently do, and a sophisticated implementation of sentiment analysis might be the key to deciphering these largely untapped texts.

Because central banks have broad influence over the entire market, our examination will cover more than the fixed-income space or the equity markets. This bigger picture will allow us to better portray the breadth of influence central banks wield over the market with their words. By virtue of engaging in such an expansive investigation, these chapters afford an informed perspective, presenting a catalogue of data on the many of the world's biggest market movers.

In a post-crisis world, central banks as whole—not just the Fed—have taken on an unprecedented position of economic leadership and market power. Fortunately, this power and position have come hand in hand with transparency, a trending strategy that not only frames the increasingly powerful moves central banks make but is, in its own right, policy itself. Transparency is here to stay, and the financial professionals that are best able to build their operations around its impact add an essential element to their understanding of global finance.

* * *

Born in 1957, the European Union (EU) was formed to unite the European economy, a cohesion its founders hoped to achieve through the creation of " a 'common market' for trade" (European Commission 2015). It wasn't long, however, before the EU member states realized that as powerful as the potential this vision held was—actual realization would be a lengthy process (European Commission 2015). As the European Commission's official account elaborates, "Over time it became clear that closer economic and monetary co-operation was needed for the internal market to develop and flourish further, and for the whole European economy to perform better, bringing more jobs and greater prosperity for Europe" (European Commission 2015).

Their solution? The euro. In the early 1990s the EU decided that the missing piece was "a strong and stable currency for the 21st century" (European Commission 2015). While it would take more than a decade for the physical manifestations of Europe's innovative currency make their way into wallets, the euro became tradable on the markets within eight years. As the euro phased in, the EU became united under one currency, and the eurozone was afforded a more robust, efficient unit of exchange. The European Commission's own words echo these sentiments: "Single currency makes the euro area an attractive region for third countries to do business, thus promoting trade and investment. Prudent economic management makes the euro an attractive reserve currency for third countries, and gives the euro area a more powerful voice in the global economy" (European Commission 2015). Backed by the diversity—and strength—of the entire European market and guided by some of the region's best economic minds, the euro is a currency that channels the character of a continent.

In order to develop this new currency, in 1998 the European Monetary Institute (EMI) was replaced by the ECB. Just like the Fed, the ECB was built to maintain a new currency. Also, just like the Fed, politics played a constant role in creation and governance of the ECB. For example, as the ECB took over the EMI's role in the late 1990s, controversy soon broke out over who should be the new central bank's president. As agreed upon by governors of the national central banks, Willem F. Duisenberg, a former Dutch central banker and head of the EMI, emerged as the first president of the ECB. The president of France, Jacques Chirac, had different ideas. Chirac felt that because the new central bank was located in Germany, it would only be fair for the new central bank president to be French. Opposing Duisenberg's nomination, he backed Jean-Claude Trichet—the head of the Banque de France—as ECB president. The Netherlands, along with Belgium and Germany, wanted a strong euro, and they felt that Duisenberg could be trusted with that charge. As the conflict mounted—especially between Chirac and Helmut Kohl, the German Chancellor—an unofficial agreement was struck: at some time during his eight-year term, Duisenberg would step down and allow Trichet step in—which he did in 2003. Beyond demonstrating the integral part politics played in the birth of this central bank, the incident also offers valuable insight into challenges that attend the management of the ECB: in addition to the challenges that all central banks face, the ECB is charged with the unenviable task of navigating the numerous historical, cultural, and economic intricacies of a continent (Centre Virtuel de la Connaissance sur l'Europe 2012).

* * *

The ECB is managed by the Governing Council, which is comprised of the presidents of the central banks of each of the EU member states and an Executive Board. Each state gets one representative on the Council, but the president, vice president, and the Executive Board members do not go toward this count. For instance, Mario Draghi was the Bank of Italy's president, but because Draghi is the ECB's current president, Italy has an additional Council member: Ignazio Visco. As of 2015, 6 Executive Board members and 19 representatives from the other central banks in the EU populate the council. Like in the Fed, the Executive Board members have more direct influence over monetary policy than do the 19 representatives. The guiding hand behind the eurozone's economy, this Council discusses and implements new monetary policy and sets the rates at which financial institutions can borrow money from the central bank (European Central Bank 2015a).

Interestingly, the ECB shares some structural similarities with private companies. For instance, shares in the central bank can be purchased; ECB stock, however, can only be purchased by states. The total value of the ECB's capital stock is 10.8 billion euros, and national central banks both within and outside the EU own stock in the ECB. Of this, the majority is owned by euro nations, some nations owning more than others—Germany owns almost 18 percent of the stock and France owns just over 14 percent. These ownership percentages are fixed, as the stock in the ECB is meant to reflect each nation's position in the euro area. The population and economic production of each member state relative to the entire area, weighted in equal parts, are what determine this percentage. For example, if a country's gross domestic product (GDP) and total population represented, respectively, 30 and 20 percent of the euro area, then that country would be allowed to maintain a 25 percent ownership of the ECB's capital stock. This policy insures that the ECB is truly representative of the economic and social realities of the region it serves and that the central bank is secured from "political influence" (Deutsche Bundesbank 2014).

While the Fed has its dual mandate to keep inflation low and employment at a maximum, the ECB (like most other central banks) only has one primary objective: to maintain price stability. Price stability, in terms of the ECB's charge, is defined as euro inflation rates that approach, but do not exceed, 2 percent (a target that is likely more politically than economically motivated). The ECB relies on what they call refinancing operations—main refinancing operations (MROs) and long-term refinancing operations (LTROs)—to achieve this stability. The monetary levers the ECB manipulates to accomplish its ends are quite similar to some of those that the Fed employs to guide the US economy: the main refinancing rate, that will be touched on now, and the marginal lending rate, that will be discussed later, that power MROs are much like the Fed funds rate and the Fed discount window, respectively.

The ECB regularly conducts MROs in order to, according the ECB, "steer short-term interest rates, to manage the liquidity situation and to signal the monetary policy stance in the euro area" (European Central Bank 2015b). In an MRO, the ECB allots capital in an auction where banks compete for the short-term loans, and those banks offer higher rates receive funds until the total amount offered for auction is exhausted. Through its own analysis of market conditions, the ECB determines the amount it should offer up in these auctions. The ECB executes LTROs as a complement to its MROs, by providing "additional, longer-term refinancing to the financial sector" (European Central Bank 2015b). While MRO loans come in two-week and one-month terms, LTRO loans range from three months to three years (Financial Times 2015b). By altering the supply of capital to banks, the ECB uses these loans affect interest rates and liquidity, while simultaneously communicating the economic aims of the ECB.

* * *

The ECB has been active in the aftermath of the global financial crisis, cutting interest rates by injecting an unprecedented amount of capital into the system in an effort to push the euro market out of the recession. After a short stint of interest rate hikes in 2011—the first since 2008—the ECB began to dramatically cut rates in the following years. From 2012 to 2013 the ECB sharply lowered interest rates to encourage economic growth, reaching the historically low 0.25 percent in November 2013. Historic as that rate was, the bar would continue to drop. Soon after the rates were cut to 0.15 percent, and then, in September of 2014 the central bank reduced the rates by two-thirds from 0.15 percent to 0.05 percent, the lowest rates on record—one that the ECB has held since as of this writing.

To accomplish its record-setting interest rates, the ECB has expanded the tools in its policymaking toolbox. Usually, MROs, like those mentioned above, offer a limited amount of capital to competing financial institutions, but the depth of the crisis has required unusual tactics: to increase liquidity depleted by the subprime mortgage crisis, the ECB lowered interest rates to levels before unseen in the euro area and provided substantial credit support through the Securities Markets Programme (European Central Bank 2010).

This diffused tension in several markets, the money market included. As such, since October 2008, the ECB has conducted several MROs on a fixed basis where amounts are fully allotted at a fixed interest rate—the marginal lending rate. The additional funds provided via the marginal lending rate by the ECB come at a higher interest rate than what is available in the interbank market, but it allows financial firms to overcome problems engendered by scarce liquidity without facing the high costs associated with near or full insolvency.

Most recently, even these generous liquidity injections haven't served to stir a sluggish European economy out of the doldrums, and the central bank has moved to take even more direct, dramatic action. Lifting a play straight from the Fed's game plan, the ECB has embracing quantitative easing (QE) as part of their continued rescue efforts. In early 2015, the ECB began implementing the 1 trillion dollar initiative, but even before the policy's tires met the road, the announcement of the plan sent stock markets into ecstasy, propelling the FTSEurofirst 300, an index of the 300 largest European companies ranked by market cap, to its highest close since before the financial crisis (Robinson 2015).

The primary objective of the recent QE initiative is to combat a disinflationary euro by pushing inflation back up to near 2 percent to catalyze consumption. The trillion euro prescription will come in monthly injections of 60 billion euros until the fall of 2016, each wave set to buy up swathes of troubled sovereign debt (Buttonwood 2015). Initial signs, beyond the announcement excitement, are positive: "Growth forecasts have been continually revised up since January when the program was announced: the International Monetary Fund said this week it now expects the eurozone to grow by 1.5% in 2015. Business and consumer confidence are the highest since 2007. Bank lending is finally picking up" (Nixon 2015).

* * *

It's important to note that the reason the ECB has taken so long to implement QE measures is due to particular scope of the central bank's powers. When it comes to open market operations, the ECB's toolbox is—compared to banks like the Fed—limited. Consequently, the legality of the asset purchasing needed to implement QE was unclear, and, because of this, the ECB has had to inch toward these policies.

* * *

Along with groundbreaking and sweeping monetary policy, transparency is another staple of a post-crisis ECB. In no uncertain terms, Mario Draghi has recently asserted the centrality—and continued expansion—of the role of open communication in the central bank's ongoing strategy:

> More recently, we have decided to go one step further and to publish regular accounts of Governing Council monetary policy discussions, starting with the meeting on 21–22 January 2015, the account of which was published last Thursday. Through these accounts, we are enriching the communication of the rationale behind our monetary policy decisions and seek to give a sense of the discussion that has taken place among Governing Council members and the main arguments that were exchanged. We believe that this will enable members of the public and markets to improve their understanding of our assessment of the economy and our policy responses in the light of evolving conditions, our so-called "reaction function." In the current circumstances, it will also underpin our forward guidance on interest rates. It will thereby further enhance the effectiveness of our monetary policy. (Draghi 2015)

Given the history of market reaction to central banking communications—the stock market reaction to the QE announcement being just one example—European central bankers are looking to leverage transparency as tool to bolster the other elements of their monetary policy.

This development is especially significant given the power the ECB wields. In fact, the singularly prominent position the ECB holds in the eurozone (collectively the largest economy in the world) gives their word more impact on the economy it oversees than, perhaps, any other central bank outside of the Fed. This power is, in part, the product of the nature of the currency it commands. As the guardian of the euro, the ECB holds the keys to the currency that to unite the European market and, therefore, is the salient force behind the financial fate of the continent.

But the ECB's authority extends far beyond the European economy. If, for example, the ECB decides to pursue inflationary policy, devaluing the euro in relation to outside currencies, it becomes less expensive for foreign buyers to purchase European goods and services because their dollar, yen, yuan, etc., go further—and it simultaneously becomes more costly for Europeans to buy outside their market. If the converse is true, and the ECB enacts disinflationary monetary policy, then eurozone goods become comparatively more expensive—dissuading exports—while the stronger euro makes foreign goods cheaper—encouraging imports. Thus, the ECB has a broad influence on the both economy of the EU member states—which have total population exceeding 330 million (US Census Bureau 2014; European Union 2015)—and the economies of any other nation that would aspire to do business within the eurozone.

* * *

That said, how does the data bear out this influence? Capturing the ten-year bond yield and our sentiment data on the ECB, Figure 11.1 provides an illustration of the effect ECB communications have on the European fixed-income markets.

In Figure 11.1, the ten-year bond yield is portrayed in dots and dashes, and the ECB Index is represented by the broken line. The

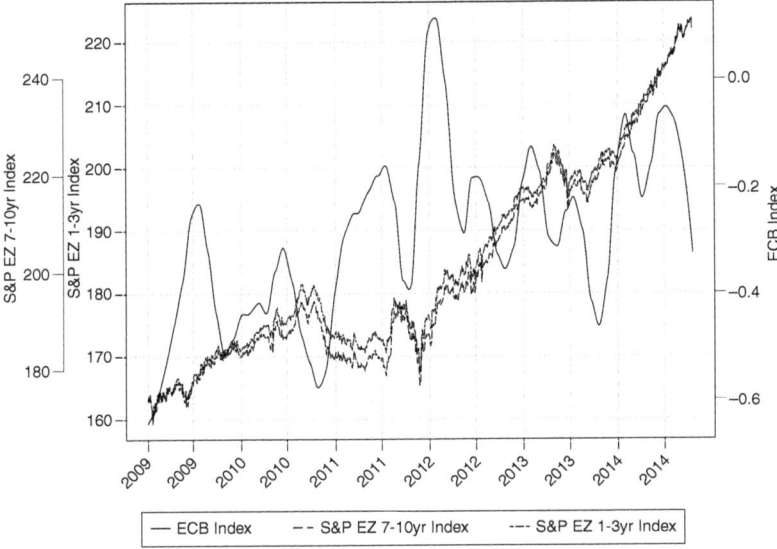

Figure 11.1 ECB Index and the ECB ten-year bond yield.

ECB's sentiment and fixed income do seem to share a correlation—but an inverse correlation. As the central bank's sentiment trends upwards from dovish to neutral, the bold yield declines, and each data stream seems to hit its high just as the other hits its low. The end of 2011 to the beginning of 2014 is a particularly illustrative of this inverse relationship: late 2011-to-early 2011 sees the ECB Index trend rise sharply, and this spike is inversely manifested in the bond yield's steep downward shift; 2013 sees both trends reverse simultaneously, culminating in an intersection that occurs late in the year. This mirroring dynamic suggests that there could be a causal relationship between the central bank's economic position and the fixed income market, and this relationship could be used by financial professionals as an indicator for market development—an upward trend in the ECB Index would seem to suggest an incoming downward movement in the ten-year bond yield—and could also be indicative of movements in the fixed-income market as a whole.

In the fixed income markets, the ECB's mood does seem to have a recognizable effect on market outcomes. Given these promising results, further investigations leveraging the insight afforded by our methodology could certainly help shed additional light on the complex fluctuations in the eurozone economy.

* * *

As the ECB's mood seems to illuminate aspects of fixed-income market activity, perhaps a similar relationship can be found between the ECB Index and the European equity markets. As Figure 11.2 demonstrates, the ECB's mood clearly impacts equity markets.

In Figure 11.2, the S&P Euro 350 is represented by the broken and dotted line, the Euro STOXX 50 by the broken line, and the ECB Index by the solid black line. The movements of the ECB Index—while more volatile than the market—share a predictive relationship with the indexes, climbing and diving with market fluctuations. For instance, market highs like those seen in mid-2011, late 2013 and mid-2014 are consistently correlated with or anticipated by Index peaks, demonstrating the utility of central bank communications as an indicator of market developments.

This notable relationship seems perfectly reasonable once the nature of ECB communications and open market activity is considered. If, for example, the ECB communications begin trending

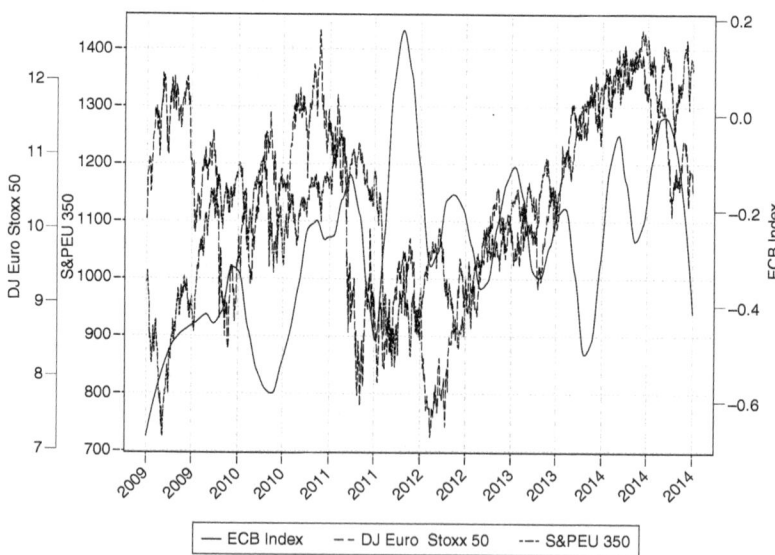

Figure 11.2 ECB Index and European equities indexes.

more hawkish, two signals are sent to market actors. The first signal is that inflation is on the rise—a trend that usually signals accelerated economic growth. A firm will use this first signal to react to increasing inflation, which may include capitalizing on the increase or preventing losses due to the increase, depending on the firm's strategy and risk tolerance. This could be a reason why we still see market growth after hawkish statements. The second signal is that the ECB may soon contract the money supply to stymie inflation. A firm will react to this signal separately—ECB action contracting the money supply may induce divestment from equity, and investment in currency hedged assets as the euro begins to appreciate. This policy implementation is likely why the market contracts within a four- to six-month window after the communication. The question in the second case is, then, if or when the ECB will actually take action, and the ECB Index can serve as a leading indicator of these future actions. The sentiment indicator discriminates between degrees of hawkishness—as the index becomes more extreme, action will be imminent or more severe. This same dynamic works in the opposite order for dovish policy. This means ECB communications can be expected to have a predictive relationship with the equity market, and these expectations, like many others that have been discussed in this book, seem to be vindicated by the data.

* * *

While a relatively new player on the global stage, the ECB is an unquestioned leader among its peers, because what the ECB lacks in legacy it makes up for in power. Its authority over the euro—the money that unifies a population and economy larger than that of the United States—grants the ECB this clear sway (and say) in this robust and diverse economy and, by connection, the rest of the world. As it has been with the Fed, this authority finds itself increasingly expressed through communications, and, as it also was with the Fed, these (escalating) developments suggest the need for hard data on the role ECB communications play in financial markets. Utilizing our proprietary method of sentiment analysis, we have been able to generate this hard data on the market-moving behemoth, producing a quantitative analysis of ECB texts that could serve as the standard for central bank watching in Europe, just as it does in the United States.

12

BOE Sentiment: The Origin of Modern Central Bank Communications

Banking history is, as a rule, not the most commonly researched topic, but even a casual investigation reveals that central banking has a long tradition maintaining financial stability, and the Bank of England (BOE) stands as exhibit A to that point. Chartered in 1694, the BOE is one of the oldest central banks on earth, and this established institution has, like many central banks, only gained authority and economic prominence over its reign. This chapter begins by looking into the long history of one of the first central banks in the world, tracing the evolution of an institution—from monetary lightweight to undisputed powerhouse—that helped build an empire. Like with the Fed and the ECB, the BOE's rise to financial authority has been followed by an equally significant measure of transparency, and it is this thread, as in other chapters, that is examined the most in this one. In its entire history, the BOE has never looked so lively—or been so vocal—a simultaneous development that makes what the central bank has to say more consequential than ever before.

* * *

The history of any central bank is ultimately tied to the history of its currency. Federal Reserve notes were born with the Federal Reserve System. The European Central Bank was created to oversee the fledgling euro. Almost any account of a central bank is incomplete without first examining the story of the money with which it keeps account, and, therefore, our introduction to BOE doesn't begin with buildings or bricks; it begins with pounds.

The pound gets its name from a very logical source: its weight. In the ancient Anglo-Saxon world—over 1,200 years ago—silver coins, later known as "sterlings," were the common money (Dawnay 2001). Two hundred and forty sterlings weighed a pound, and the measurement became an easy title for what is now the world's oldest active currency (Dawnay 2001; Rendall 2007). Almost 1,000 years later the BOE was established to help manage the pound, produce banknotes (guarantees used for money and backed by precious metals), and finance England's war against France (Dawnay 2001). While certainly wielding significant monetary authority, the central bank did not, at first, have a monopoly on currency production; banks in Ireland, Scotland, and Wales also had the legal authority to produce paper money, and it would be more than 100 years before the BOE became the exclusive producer and guardian of English money (Dawnay 2001). The Bank Charter Act in 1844 made the BOE the sole monetary authority in the United Kingdom and established firm standards for the currency that the central bank would now have exclusive power over. Backing every note with gold, the BOE would maintain the integrity of the pound, guard the gold reserves, and be the lender of last resort for banks in trouble. What followed was a period of remarkable prosperity for England, as the strength of the currency powered the golden hue of Victorian England's global reach (Dawnay 2001). But the expenses of World War I saw the gold standard wobble, and, by the early 1930s, England fully abandoned it (Dawnay 2001). Even though the pound was listed alongside dollar as a reserve currency by the Bretton Woods Agreement, by that time it was clear that the currency's best years were behind it—the title of "reserve currency" was more of a political gesture than an actual indication of economic reality.

* * *

Today, the BOE and its operations are managed by an Executive Team and several committees. The Executive Team, which serves as the most powerful guiding hand in the institution, is composed of a governor, four deputy governors, a chief operating officer, and a crew of executive directors. The deputy governors are each assigned specific charges that account for the majority of the BOE's mandated tasks: there are deputy governors for Monetary Policy, Markets and Banking, Financial Stability, and Prudential Regulation Authority. The deputy governors work hand in hand with the governor, who oversees—and is responsible for—the progress of the entire bank. While attending to these fundamental BOE duties, the governors are the bank's ambassadors, speaking on a wide variety of economic issues before local and global audiences (Bank of England 2015). Interestingly, the BOE has a longstanding tradition of having a foreigner serve as one of the deputy governors to insure legitimacy—a practice which has its roots in the pound's former place as a global reserve currency. Responsible for the management of human resources, IT, and security, the COO directs the operational essentials of the BOE, while the executive directors, the final part of the Executive team, head up communications, human resources, finance, and the many other departments integral to a modern central bank.

The BOE has four important committees—the Court, the Monetary Policy Committee, the Financial Policy Committee, and the Prudential Regulation Authority—and the governor of BOE is integral member of all these committees. The Court, which is the BOE's board of directors, is responsible for all the bank's operations outside of monetary policy, handling matters like the budget, risk management policies, and the bank's objectives (Bank of England 2015). The Monetary Policy Committee determines and sets interest rates to reach the BOE's inflation targets; the Financial Policy Committee works to strengthen the United Kingdom's economy by targeting and eliminating risk in the financial system; and the Prudential Regulation Authority—much like the FDIC in the United States—oversees and regulates banking (Bank of England 2015). Together, these committees help protect the British financial system through the implementation of calculated measures to cultivate growth and mitigate economic crises.

* * *

When it was founded 1694, the BOE was charged to "promote the public good and benefit of our people" and its current statement of purpose—"to promote the good of the people of the United Kingdom by maintaining monetary and financial stability"—is not, as the BOE has noted, all that different from the motto that christened it over 300 years ago (Bank of England 2015). The BOE cultivates financial stability by maintaining the efficient flow of funds in the economy and upholding the public's confidence in their financial institutions, and it pursues these ends through its standard financial operations, oversight of financial market infrastructures (FMIs), and management of its major committees. A standard duty of any central bank is to support the market by operating as a lender of last resort. By offering loans to banks that cannot meet the demands of depositors or their reserve requirements, the BOE backs not only these important institutions but their customers as well, bolstering the pillars of the financial system. Along with securing these economic moorings, the BOE also monitors the mechanisms of trade. FMIs, like payment and securities settlement systems, are integral to the smooth movement of money through the economy. To insure that these systems are running properly with the appropriate attention to risk management, especially in regards to the wider scope of the entire financial system, the BOE closely supervises their operation (Bank of England 2015). Committed to combating the numerous dangers that plague economic enterprise, the Financial Policy Committee (FPC) has been "given tough powers to tame systemic risk by clamping down on loose credit, overheated sectors and previously unregulated parts of the financial system" (Bank of England 2015). The final piece of this arsenal, the Prudential Regulations Authority, compliments the FPC's oversight of the Financial Market Infrastructures with its supervision of over 1,500 financial institutions like banks, credit unions, and investment firms (Bank of England 2015). Through its thorough vetting of fundamental market mechanics and its power to extend emergency financing, the BOE is the watchdog of the United Kingdom's economic stability.

To accomplish its charge of monetary stability, the BOE seeks to maintain both price stability and confidence in its currency, and the bank attempts to fulfill both through the careful control of the inflation rate. This rate, which has been set by the government, is 2 percent—a target chosen because it is believed to avoid the overheating that excess inflation can cause while providing a cushion from the economic stagnation that can come from a deflationary currency. The 2 percent rate, in other words, is thought to keep inflation low enough to maintain consumer confidence in the pound as a useful means of trade and wealth preservation, while, at the same time, to be depreciative enough to stimulate the purchase of goods and services and catalyze economic growth. While the relatively straightforward thinking behind inflation targeting seems sound, the unpredictability and complexity of the global economy cast strong doubt on whether such policies can deliver on their stated goals (Schnidman 2012). In reality, such targets are more political moves than actual policy.

* * *

By attempting to encouraging economic growth—bolstering trade and employment—and maintaining price stability, the BOE's objectives are reminiscent (though less explicit) of the Fed's own dual mandate, and the BOE's most recent initiatives also run parallel to the US central bank. In early 2009, the BOE began its own round of quantitative easing because interest rates were already low, and the central bank needed another means of hitting their goal of 2 percent inflation. In order to support these novel initiatives, the BOE has made a concerted effort to use forward guidance to improve the lines of communication between itself and the public. This resurgence in the central bank's commitment to transparency could give the impression that open communication is a recent development BOE, but nothing could be further from the truth. In fact, the BOE, as was mentioned with an earlier chapter, was actually among the first to incorporate this strategy into its operations:

> Before it was fashionable, the Bank of England (Bank) was an early pioneer in the pursuit of transparency. In 1993, the institution became the first among its peers to publish an inflation report. The Bank renewed its transparency efforts after it was granted operational independence from Her Majesty's Government in 1997. The newly created Monetary Policy Committee (MPC) was determined to build a strong public constituency in support of its price stability mandate. In the aftermath of the global financial crisis, the Bank's policies and practices were subjected to even

greater scrutiny, not least in the realm of transparency. In its 2014 Strategic Plan, the Bank reaffirmed its commitment to openness and accountability, and expressed its aspiration to enhance its transparency further. (Warsh 2014)

Just as it is the case with Federal Reserve and the European Central Bank, transparency has become a critical asset for the BOE as it attempts to handle the economic challenges and criticisms that have accompanied its decisions—especially since the crisis. As emphasized by the passage above, this openness has been especially integral to the BOE's price goals as the institution attempts to mitigate misinterpretation and, therefore, negative outcomes by informing the public of underlying strategy of economic balance. Since July of 2012, the BOE has ceased quantitative easing (QE) asset purchasing, and, by that time, the BOE had injected more QE funds per capita than any other central bank in the world through the financial crisis. The BOE has continued to aggressively implement monetary stimulus in their policy, and forward guidance has remained firmly in place as a powerful tool of policy to shape public perception and implement these vital initiatives.

* * *

These developments make the BOE an ideal candidate for our proprietary method of sentiment analysis. Because the BOE was a pioneer of transparency, we have access to a much larger set of documents than we do with most central banks, and this abundance of material affords our analytical program with the breadth of history needed for it to achieve a higher level of scoring accuracy. This long history of open communication also means that the BOE itself has had more time to hone its reporting practices, making them more likely to utilize a carefully curated vocabulary when explaining their economic aims. This also directly affects the quality of the signal our interpretive methods are able to produce: the more consistent any central bank is with its terminology, the more reliable our scoring becomes.

While transparency has certainly had a significant history in the BOE, in the greater picture, the central bank is treading into uncharted economic territory. The coupling of incredibly low interest rates with equally low inflation rates along with the BOE's relatively recent use of QE and increasing emphasis on forward guidance have, altogether, created a brave new world of finance in Britain. These developments have changed the game for financial analysts, who can no longer draw upon familiar resources to inform their projections (Peters 2014). All this means that financial professionals with a vested interest in the UK market are in need of new signals anchored in these recent developments—developments that are increasingly involved with central bank policies.

* * *

But can analytics on BOE communications really offer insight into the UK economy? Our sentiment data on the central bank serves affords a means appraisal. Figure 12.1 lays the BOE Index alongside the indexes of the Financial Times Stock Exchange and the NASDAQ, demonstrating the relationship between BOE communications and the equities market.

If BOE communications are, in part, responsible for market fluctuations, how can this dynamic be expected to play out? If, for

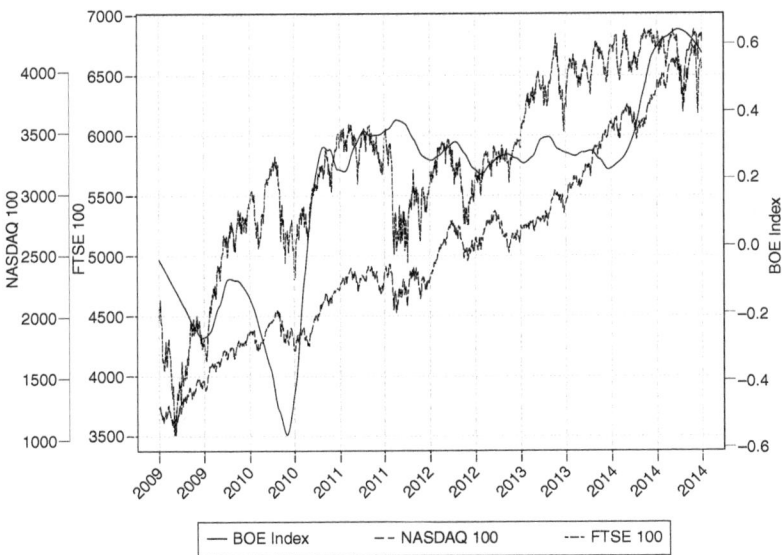

Figure 12.1 BOE Index, FTSE 100, and NASDAQ.

example, a BOE communication reflects a hawkish mood—indicating the incoming implementation of contractionary monetary policy—it could be expected that in the immediate to near future equity markets would rise and then, as the wheels of policy take effect, begin to fall. The markets—or at least those segments influenced by watchful market actors—could be predicted to rise after a hawkish communication because a hawkish stance is indicative of a growing economy and an inflationary currency, and some market actors, in light of these circumstances, would likely want to transfer their asset holdings from currency hedged assets to domestic equities to ride the market expansion. As contractionary monetary policy begins to be implemented, however, currency begins to gain value relative to other assets and the opposite strategy becomes preferable; holders of domestic equity might want to sell these assets in order to gain from the ensuing spike in the value of money, negatively impacting the performance of the stock market.

In Figure 12.1, the BOE Index is the solid black line; the NASDAQ is the broken line; and the Financial Times Stock Exchange 100 Index (FTSE) is the broken and dotted line. (Despite the fact that Britain is a technologically advanced economy, it doesn't have a substantial tech index; however, the close ties between British and US economies make the NASDAQ a useful proxy). Upon review of the figure, the expected relationship between BOE sentiment and the market performance seems to play out. In almost every instance, a peak in the BOE Index (indicating a strong market and a weak currency) is shortly followed by an uptick in market performance and, within a three-to-six-month time horizon, a dip, as market actors shift strategies in response to monetary contraction. This same relationship is seen, as might also be expected, as the BOE trends dovish. Sentiment declines are predictive of market dives—and later gains.

It may seem odd at first that the NASDAQ and the BOE Index are correlated just as the FTSE and the BOE Index are, but upon deeper reflection, this dynamic seems justified. Because (as was mentioned above) the British and US economies are tightly linked, the fact that the NASDAQ also seems to share a relationship with BOE dispatches shouldn't come as a surprise. In fact, this could also be in part due to an interaction between the communications of the banks themselves. Still, this only underscores how useful the BOE Index can be when predicting changes in the equities market—especially when combined with other sources of sentiment data, such as the Fed Index.

* * *

To further test the effectiveness of the BOE Index, we ran a backtest using the data as the sole trade indicator for an entirely equity portfolio. As a means of comparison, we have set the BOE Index-driven portfolio alongside a control: a buy-and-hold portfolio comprised of identical assets.

In Figure 12.2, the BOE Index-managed portfolio is represented by the solid black line; the buy-and-hold portfolio is represented by the broken line. Like earlier backtests, our trading decisions are informed by momentum-based strategy with thresholds adjusted to suit the particular history of the central bank communication

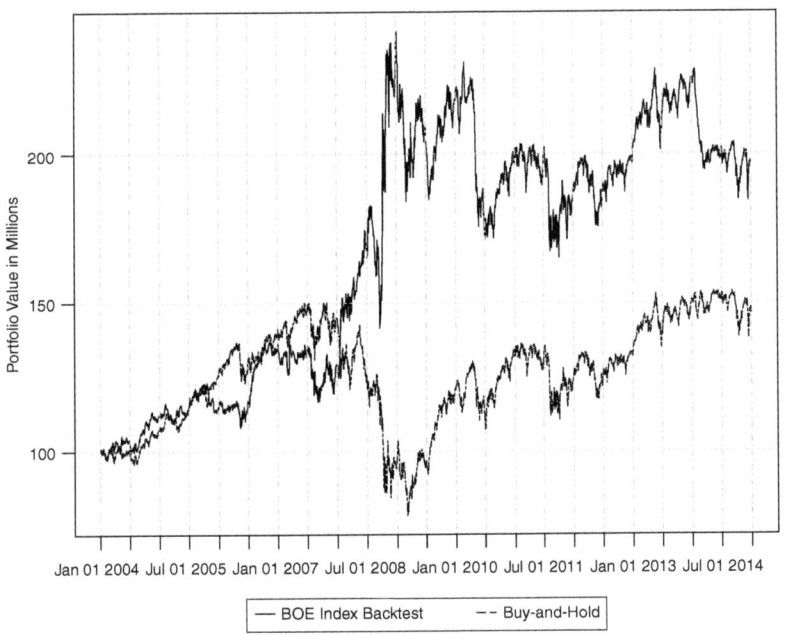

Figure 12.2 BOE Index portfolio against buy-and-hold.

trends in use. In this case, momentum changes at or above the 70th percentile would prompt a long trading move and momentum changes at or below the 40th percentile would prompt a short trading move. Beginning with an initial value of 100,000 dollars in 2004, the BOE index-managed portfolio landed at a final value of 208,161 dollars in 2014. This final value represents a remarkable return over the buy-and-hold portfolio, outperforming the control by 61 percent. Furthermore, the risk-adjusted returns demonstrate a sharp ratio of 2.289. The BOE Index's superiority over buy-and-hold is particularly evident from 2008 to 2010, when the sentiment-driven portfolio hits highs—overcoming the financial crisis—while the buy-and-hold portfolio plummets. This indicates that portfolios that the BOE Index can not only generate significant investment gains in growing market, but also withstand (and even perform) in the harshest of economic conditions.

* * *

Both in theory and in practice, the connection between the BOE's words and the economy that it serves is significant. As the BOE takes on an even greater position of market leadership and continues to push toward higher levels of frank discourse about its monetary policy, it can only be expected that this impact will continue to grow. For financial professionals, academics, or anyone looking to understand the economy, this development has made it imperative that they get a handle on the burgeoning role BOE communications play. By providing quantitative data on these texts bolstered by the bank's history of transparency, our methodology can help unlock the world's oldest central bank for today's forward-thinking finance minds.

13

BOJ Sentiment: Monetary Clues in Lost Decades

Japan and industry are almost synonymous. Home to Toyota, Mitsubishi, Honda, and Hitachi, Japan's list of major companies seems almost endless. And so does the nation's commitment to work: so many Japanese have died from their workload that the tragic circumstance has been given its own word. While the level of dedication shown by some of its workforce is almost unfathomable, what is very concrete is the country's place in the global market: the tiny island nation is home to the world's third largest national economy. As familiar as it may be today, Japan was certainly not always the economic powerhouse it is today. In a historic economic achievement that can, perhaps, only be described as miraculous, over hundred years ago, over the course of a handful of decades, Japan transformed its insular, fledgling market—one far outpaced by much of the developed world—into an undisputed engine of production.

The push that accelerated the Japanese economy also birthed the institution that now leads it: the Bank of Japan (BOJ). Like so many of the economies this book has investigated, Japan's is guided by the watchful hand and careful words of its central bank, and the main thrust of this chapter is an exploration of its mechanisms of monetary manipulation—with emphasis, of course, on the role its communications play. Serving as a trusted voice over almost two decades of economic struggle, BOJ communications deserve a dedicated investigation. Leveraging the same methodology we have used to examine the market-moving texts of the Fed, the ECB, and the BOE, this chapter subjects the BOJ's communication to the same scrutiny to discover if its language holds the same significance for financial professionals.

* * *

In 1882, the BOJ was established as part of the nationwide push towards modernization. The BOJ, which is called the "Nippon Ginko" in Japanese ("Nichigin" for short), is primarily overseen by the Policy Board. The Policy Board has nine members—the governor, currently Haruhiko Kuroda (2013–present), two deputy governors, and six additional members—and is the highest decision-making body in the Nichigin. The Policy Board "determines the guideline for currency and monetary control, sets the basic principles for carrying out the Bank's operations, and oversees the fulfillment of the duties of the Bank's officers, excluding Auditors and Counsellors" (Bank of Japan 2015). To assist the governors, the BOJ has six executive directors that are charged with handling the business operations of the BOJ and, along with the deputy governors, overseeing the Management and Compliance Committees. The Management Committee examines, contains, and solves bank-wide issues, and the Compliance Committee insures that Nichigin officers operate with due respect to relevant laws and regulations. Like the ECB, the BOJ issues stock, 55 percent of which is required to be government owned—the rest, unlike the ECB, can be privately held and is traded publicly on the JASDAQ (The Bank of Japan Act 2007). Like most central banks, the BOJ attends to a laundry list of economic chores: it issues and manages bank notes; it provides settlement services; it compiles data, research, and economic analysis; and it insures the stability of the financial system through the implementation of monetary policy. As it currently stands, the BOJ is one of the most organized and progressive central banks on earth—a truly remarkable status given that when it was established, Japan was only just breaking free of feudalism and lagged far behind the political and industrial progress seen in the West.

* * *

In 1854, the Japanese economy was first fully opened to Western commerce by the Tokugawa Shogunate—the final military government of feudal Japan—and education was an integral part of this transformative process. Sending students to the United States and other Western universities, Japan imported the thought capital—along with the weapons, technologies, culture, and lifestyle—of the Western world. The introduction of modern methods into the long insulated empire revolutionized their economy, rocketing into the nation into industrialism. It seems fitting that was during this period of rapid growth and modernization, a period referred to as the Meiji Restoration, that the BOJ was founded.

As a military power and machine of production, Japan continued its aggressive expansion until World War II. The unprecedented violence that this global conflict produced leveled Japanese cities, killed hundreds of thousands of citizens, and crippled its economic productive capacity. After the war was lost in 1945, the United States occupied the nation until 1952, during which time the Diet, the Japanese legislature, was established. This period of intense rebuilding—an effort that was significantly bolstered by US aid—allowed Japanese economy to regain traction and grow throughout the following decades. Japan was becoming an economic powerhouse, and their success had made them the envy of West.

This ascension was formally recognized by their participation in 1985's Plaza Accord. During the first half of the Reagan administration, Volker's stagflation fighting monetary policy had caused the dollar to appreciate dramatically against the Deutsche mark, the French franc, the British pound, and the Japanese yen (Brook, Sedillot and Ollivaud 2004). While a strong dollar has some upsides, this development had hurt the performance of American industry globally, and a meeting was arranged among important global economies. After the wreckage of World War II, Japan's inclusion in this process was a clear signal that the island nation had become a vital global market player.

* * *

In the 1990s, in a period known as the Lost Decade, Japan's economy nearly collapsed due to a bevy of financial issues—not the least of were morbidly overvalued assets—and the nation continued to struggle well into the 2000s. On the heels of 2011's Tōhoku earthquake and tsunami—a devastating pair of disasters that rocked Japan and cost tens of thousands of lives and hundreds of billions of dollars—the BOJ was called upon by the Japanese government to be part of a sweeping vision to revitalize a struggling nation (Ishiguro and Kitamura 2011). Abenomics, as the plan was referred to, was

> the name given to a suite of measures introduced by Japanese prime minister Shinzo Abe after his December 2012 re-election to the post he last held in 2007. His aim was to revive the sluggish economy with "three arrows": a massive fiscal stimulus, more aggressive monetary easing from the Bank of Japan, and structural reforms to boost Japan's competitiveness. (Financial Times 2015a)

As an integral part of this latest suite of economic measures, the Nichigin is obviously moving toward inflationary monetary policy, and quantitative easing, like every central bank discussed in this book up to this point, has become an essential tool for the BOJ. Initiated in 2015, the BOJ will increase its balance sheet by 15 percent of Japan's gross domestic product (GDP) per year and extend the average duration of bank purchases from 7 to 10 years. This aggressive employment of quantitative easing (QE) will continue to make the Nichigin the largest central bank, in terms of assets as a percentage of GDP, in the world.

These bold steps demonstrate the BOJ's serious commitment to fighting deflation—an unusual commitment in the world of central banking, where most institutions battle inflation instead. Regardless of its atypical nature, this effort, along with price stability, has become an essential rallying point for the central bank. But QE is not the only emergent trend in the BOJ's policy strategy. Transparency, one of the bank's two guiding principles since 1997, is also a vital facet of the modern BOJ (Bank of Japan 2015). Open communication, the BOJ's website explains, has become the essential means by which the bank maintains its independence and power:

> Regarding monetary policy, Article 3, paragraph 1 of the Bank of Japan Act stipulates that the Bank's autonomy regarding currency and monetary control shall be respected. On the other hand, considering the influence of monetary policy on the daily lives of the public, Article 3, paragraph 2 of the Act stipulates that the Bank shall endeavor to clarify to the citizen the content of its decisions, as well as its decision-making process,

regarding currency and monetary control. (Institute for Monetary and Economic Studies of the Bank of Japan 2004)

In accordance with their commitment to transparency, the BOJ regularly publishes a variety of texts on their monetary policy activities, releasing their meeting minutes, monetary policy goals, economic reviews, and various other communications to insure that the public is given a solid understanding of Nichigin policy and the conclusions that drive it (Institute for Monetary and Economic Studies of the Bank of Japan 2004). While in past years the standard policy lever was interest rates, the BOJ now finds itself turning to communication and alternative policy. As is the case with many central banks, these communications are the product of a wealth of economic data and informed opinion. Consequently, these texts are a source of considerable insight into market developments—one whose relevance continues to grow. Considering the country's 25-year economic drought and the increasingly complex and powerful monetary policy that has been put in place to deal with it, a strong handle on BOJ communications would likely to become an increasingly valuable asset to financial professionals looking for direction in a discouraging landscape.

If the Nichigin, like other major central banks, employs communication as multilayered tool of monetary policy—providing insight into the market and their incoming measures while simultaneously shaping the market it diagnosis—then can an intelligible connection between these texts and the market be made? Our method of central bank text analysis affords us the unique position to look into this pressing question, and a comparison between the BOJ Index and the Tokyo Stock Exchange (TSE) could serve as illuminating start to this investigation.

In Figure 13.1, the BOJ Index is represented by the solid black line and the Nikkei 225—a standard TSE index—is represented by the dotted and broken line. In general, the BOJ Index fluctuations correlate highly (positive 0.545) with the Nikkei 225, but, not only are the BOJ Index movements in line with Japanese equities, its peaks and valleys are nearly always predictive of (or in step with) the market's direction. This prescient relationship begins from the start of the timeline represented in the figure. In early January of 2009, as

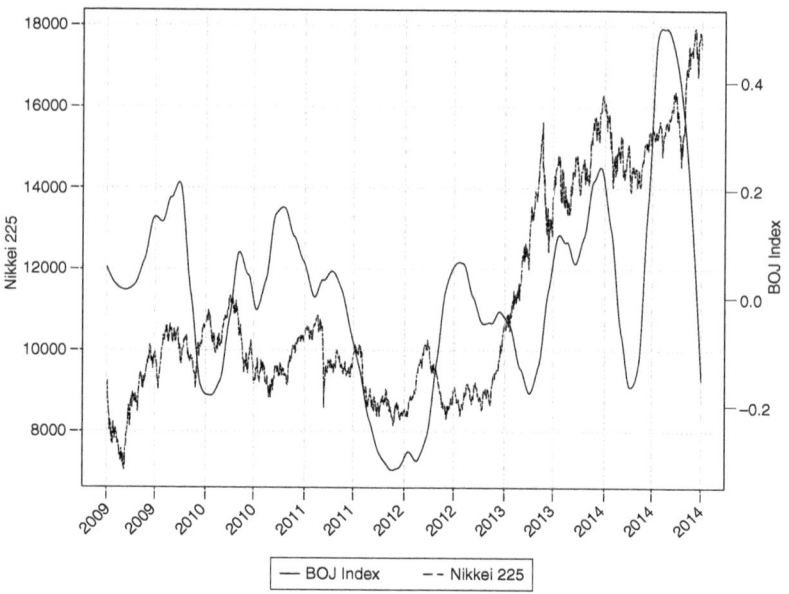

Figure 13.1 BOJ Index and the Nikkei 225.

the Nikkei is still trending downward, the BOJ Index begins almost year-long path of ascent, an upward trend that breaks only in the latter months of 2009. Approximately three months after the BOJ Index began its ascent, the Nikkei begins its own climb until the end of spring 2010, after which it descends until autumn, then once again ascends until early the following year. This entire sequence of fluctuations spanning early 2009 to the beginning of the 2011 is smoothly anticipated by the waves created by the BOJ Index, and this correlation only grows as time progresses: from the spring of 2012 onward, the BOJ Index maintains a nearly perfect four-month lead on market movements. The especially tight correlations seen in since 2012 could perhaps be linked to the adoption of Abenomics that occurred during that year, an initiative that called upon the central bank to be even more central to the economic activity of Japan. The predictive and increasingly correlative dynamic between the BOJ Index and the Nikkei suggests that BOJ communications may in fact have a pull on Japanese equities market and, in any case, suggest that the BOJ Index seems to be a valuable data stream for understanding this space.

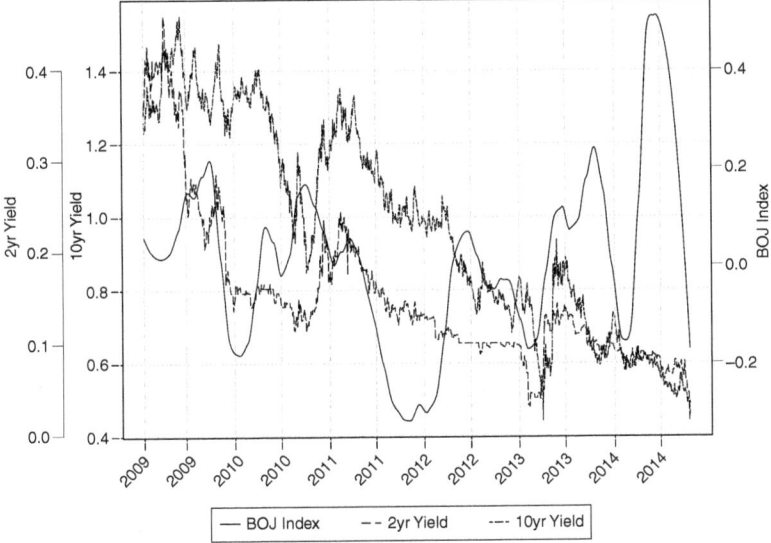

Figure 13.2 BOJ Index and Japanese government ten-year bond yield.

While this evidence seems to point to a tangible connection between the BOJ communications and equity market activity, does it suggest that a similar dynamic may exist between Nichigin texts and fixed income? An examination of the BOJ Index in relation to the benchmark ten-year Japanese Government Bond may be a useful source from which to draw observations.

In Figure 13.2, the yield on the ten-year bond is represented by the broken and dotted line and the mood of the Nichigin by the solid black line. At first glance, the relationship between the BOJ Index and the bond yield may seem weak, but a closer examination of the trends stays flash judgment. The BOJ Index is, in fact, a great indicator of future movements in the bond market—what makes that connection initially more difficult to spot is the often exaggerated nature of BOJ Index fluctuations in comparison to the rather reserved movements of this fixed-income asset. This muted market reaction could be linked to the unique dynamics of the Japanese fixed-income market. Unlike the bond markets of other major developed economies, Japanese bonds are, by and large, held domestically. This, coupled with the notoriously cautious nature of Japanese investors, could cause this market to react more slowly—and with more restraint—than other markets do toward their central bank dispatches. This dynamic is illustrated throughout the timeframe covered by the graph. For instance, from the second half of 2009 to the fall of 2010, the bond yield falls from 1.6 percent to about 0.9 percent; and, after this, the rate shoots to a high of nearly 1.3 percent in the spring of 2011 and then proceeds to gradually decrease until late 2014. The BOJ Index anticipates each of these momentum changes throughout this stretch; only its movements appear more radical. This magnified relationship is particularly noticeable from the beginning of 2011 until the middle of 2012, where the BOJ Index's trend slope is markedly steeper than the measured decline seen in the bond yield. But, for those looking for reliable market signals, the ability to project the precise angle of descent or ascent is not as important as the ability to project a coming shift in direction, and, by this criterion, the BOJ Index excels.

Like with the equity markets, the comparison of BOJ Index trends to bond yields seems indicative of a relationship—but can the same said of foreign exchange markets? While the BOJ Index and the Fed Index's relationship to the FOREX rates were covered in an earlier chapter, the potential relationship between only the BOJ Index and significant currency pairs alone has yet to be examined. A review of Figure 13.3, which sets the BOJ Index alongside the euro-yen and the USD-yen, might shed some light on that query.

The BOJ Index is represented in Figure 13.3 by the solid black line, the yen-USD by the broken and dotted line, and the yen-euro by the broken line. The yen-USD and the euro-yen closely mirror each other, with yen-euro exaggerating the movements in the yen-USD, and the BOJ Index highly correlates with the both values—0.506 with the yen-USD and 0.461 with the yen-euro to be specific. The correlation is extremely tight from early 2009 until spring-2011, when the BOJ Index dives until the beginning of 2012—serving as a leading indicator of the 2012 dive in exchange rates for the yen-euro. This ascent is shortly followed by a series of furrows and crests: the signal falls until spring of 2013, climbs until winter, falls again until just before summer of 2014, dips slightly, climbs until the late summer of 2014 and then falls sharply for the rest of the year. Impressively, each of these exaggerated movements in the BOJ Index effectively forecast (or moved with) market fluctuations.

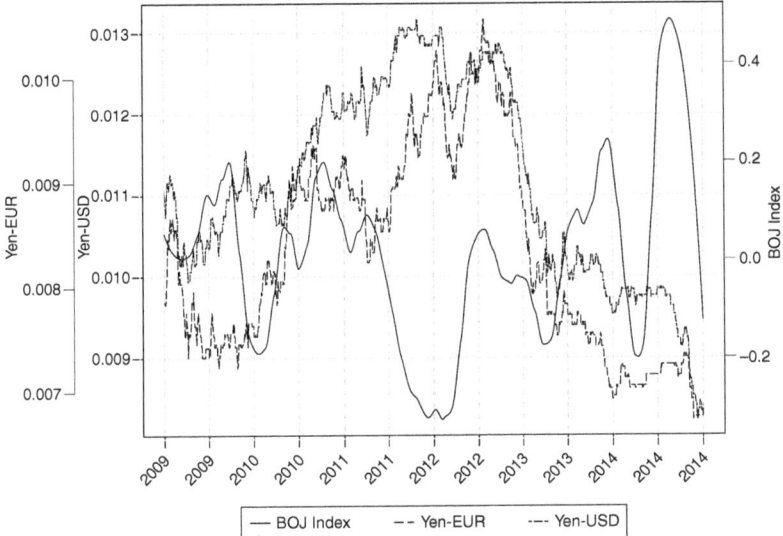

Figure 13.3 BOJ Index, yen-USD, and yen-euro.

Perhaps even more than it did with the equities market, the momentum shifts in the BOJ Index serve as reliable indicators of market fluctuations in the currency markets.

* * *

Do the Bank of Japan's communications move markets? Our examination of the BOJ Index's relationship to equity, fixed-income, and FOREX markets certainly gives that impression. Of course, the performance of any economy—especially one as massive as Japan's—is the product of innumerable moving parts, but parts that move 15 percent of GDP are about as powerful as factors come. With such an enormous economic presence, is it any wonder that when the BOJ speaks the market listens?

Indeed, when the recent trends in Japanese policy are considered together—the plan to inject the market with a massive stimulus, employ monetary easing, and engage the public through transparency measures—it seems little surprise that the data points to a central bank whose words and actions have become one. That being the case, a familiar corollary can be iterated here: understanding the modern financial landscape of Japan requires an understanding of the economic impact of BOJ's communications. But, to get a true handle on that requires a system that is able to transform Japanese characters and sentiments as they relate to market movements into meaningful, objective data points, and the program we have developed produces just that. Armed with this kind of data, financial professionals who look to engage this complex market in an informed manner have found an increasingly relevant means of coming to grips with the fluctuations of the Japanese economy and have, consequently, a greater chance to successfully navigate its ebbs and flows as they continue to push on in an environment unlike any in the country's history.

14

RBA Sentiment: Australia as a Proxy for China

This book, so far, has covered the Federal Reserve, the European Central Bank, the Bank of England, and the Bank of Japan. The economies these banks preside over all fall within the top five worldwide and, consequently, their significance to the global market is obvious. Sitting at 13th, the Australian economy has pull, but it still lags far behind the production power of the European Union, the United States, the United Kingdom, and Japan (Economy Watch 2010). With this in mind, at least one question immediately arises: why examine the Reserve Bank of Australia (RBA) alongside these other central banks when seven other, larger economies stand in line between Australia and this group? The answer lies in Australia's close ties to a market that shares the thin air occupied by that cadre of heavy-hitters: China. Beginning with a short history of the RBA, this chapter explores the relationship between the Australian and Chinese economies, highlighting how a close examination of RBA communications could provide valuable insight into two of the most powerful economies in the world.

* * *

The modern RBA evolved out of the Commonwealth Bank, an institution created just before the modern Federal Reserve—but with very limited powers (Reserve Bank of Australia 2015). Upon its founding in 1911, the Commonwealth Bank was not structurally much different from any other bank; it could not, for example, issue money or enact monetary policy. It would take several decades before the institution was fully empowered with the authority and charge that is now standard for central banks (Reserve Bank of Australia 2015), and, by the time all these powers had been granted and the bank's structure began to settle, the Commonwealth Bank had a new name as well: the RBA.

The RBA has a three-part mission: uphold the integrity of the Australian dollar, maintain full employment in country (which, outside the Fed, is an uncommon mandate), and promote the economic prosperity and welfare of its citizens. The central bank's two governing boards—the Payment Systems Board and the Reserve Bank Board—are responsible for approximating these aims. As the RBA's economic policy arm, the Reserve Bank Board generates monetary policy and maintains the stability of the Australian economy. Like many central banks, the RBA aims to maintain financial stability largely through a targeted inflation rate, which is, in this case, between 2 and 3 percent. By keeping inflation within that relatively low range, the Reserve Bank Board fights to keep the Australian dollar secure, while devaluing the currency just enough to encourage sustainable economic growth and meet their employment mandate. Along with inflation control, the other lever of monetary policy that the Reserve Bank Board utilizes is the cash rate, which, like the federal funds rate (FFR), is the interest rate on overnight loans between banks. With this rate, the RBA can work toward easing or tightening credit. The second half of this bipartite system, the Payment Systems Board, oversees the monetary rails that make transaction possible and works to insure the flow of funds between accounts is safe and efficient. By attending to the underlying plumbing of the financial system while it manipulates the monetary streams that drive economic progress, the RBA seeks to fulfill its charge as the guardian of the Australian prosperity.

* * *

But there is another (unofficial) target for the RBA that must be mentioned: the Chinese economy. Throughout the rapid expansion of the country's infrastructure, China has been in desperate need of the raw materials needed to create the buildings, roads, power supplies, and pipelines for a country of well over a billion. Because of this, China has become a massive consumer of Australian iron, coal, gold, and petroleum—the list goes on—accounting for a staggering 29 percent of country's imports (Observatory of Economic Complexity 2015). The Australian government's own economic assessment demonstrates the depth and importance China plays in the Australian economy:

> As China moves into its next phase of development, its demand will shift from raw materials to elaborately transformed manufactures, services, and expertise. Australia has some potential advantages in the supply of these, but they are not the clear advantages possessed by the resources sector. Few other countries had Australia's huge supplies of iron ore, which were close to the sea and easily developed, and proximity to China for shipping minerals (of which transport costs are up to 10% of the value). But many developed countries have the education and technical expertise to meet China's new demands. (Holmes 2015)

The vitality of the Australian economy is, therefore, powerfully linked to China's, and the RBA's monetary policy is, consequently, powerfully shaped by this dependence. So, for those hoping to understand the Australian central bank's monetary policy, the performance of the Chinese market is an essential data stream to have on hand. But this dynamic has further implications: not only is the Chinese market an important tool for understanding the thinking that drives the policy positions of the RBA, but the attitude of the RBA is essential to understanding the Chinese market and the ever-opaque Chinese central bank.

While there is data available on the Chinese financial market performance (for instance, the performance of their equities market and their government's ten-year bond yields are readily available), data on the fundamentals of the Chinese economy reflect the Chinese government's secretive stance toward the rest of the world. Nowhere is this lack of openness more apparent than in the policy of the People's Bank of China (PBoC): they are the only major central bank in the world that continues to be intentionally nontransparent. This leads to the question: how can we ascertain the intentions of a central bank or the true performance of the economy it oversees when both have been purposefully obscured? For this, a proxy is needed—a role that the Australian economy and the RBA are both well suited for.

If, for example, China begins importing vast amounts of Australian commodities, then the conclusion can be logically made that the Chinese economy is growing rapidly. In other words, Australian exports become a useful—and less biased—indicator of Chinese economic performance. From recent developments, it appears that this dynamic is here to stay (for the foreseeable future) and, therefore, can continue to be reliably counted for its use as an economic spotlight into an otherwise murky economy. This can be seen clearly in the significant investment that firms are making in Australia's booming natural resources sector—a sector that is booming in large part, if not wholly, because of its exports to China. For instance, the Export-Import Bank of the United States recently authorized a 2.95 billion dollar loan for a liquefied natural gas project in Queensland (Congressional Research Service 2013), a joint venture between enterprises from Australia, China, and the United States. This success of this project hinges on the strength of the Australia-China relationship: the United States invests in an Australian business to reap the benefits of Chinese demand, while the Chinese invest to further supply needed materials to their economy. As such, we can continue to look to Australian economic change as a proxy of Chinese economic change.

The relationship that exists between Australian economy and the Chinese economy is also present between the RBA and the Chinese economy. The RBA's monetary policy, including its communicative practices, is strongly influenced by the pull of the PBoC. In fact, China exerts a direct influence on Australia's interest rates—something normally within the purview of a nation's central bank. As the Australian government points out, "Australian businesses have benefited from low interest rates [...] driven by the large amount of Chinese savings available for lending, both directly to Australia, but also internationally" (Holmes 2015). Moreover, the Australian government anticipates that "as these are reduced, interest rates will rise, putting downward pressure on the profits of Australian businesses, revenue and growth" (Holmes 2015). Indeed, there is a case to be made for the influence of China in the RBA's decisions and, thus, communications. For financial professionals, this dynamic magnifies the importance of the RBA, making it one of the most important central banks in the world.

* * *

If current RBA monetary policy is so important—and so connected to China—what has recent monetary policy been? In the early months of 2015, the Australian central bank began tapering off some of its easing measures due to fears that continued easing might lead to an overheated economy. Because communication is also a tool of monetary policy, the position of RBA sentiment also serves as a useful metric for understanding the central bank's recent positions. As shown in Figure 14.1 alongside the standard Australian equities index—the Australian Securities Exchange (ASX) 500—the Reserve Bank of Australia Index (RBA Index), like the tapering measures, points to a hawkish RBA.

The RBA Index, represented by the solid black line, rose dramatically from 2009 to the beginning of 2011—and continues to hover in hawkish values afterward. But, considering the situation, this

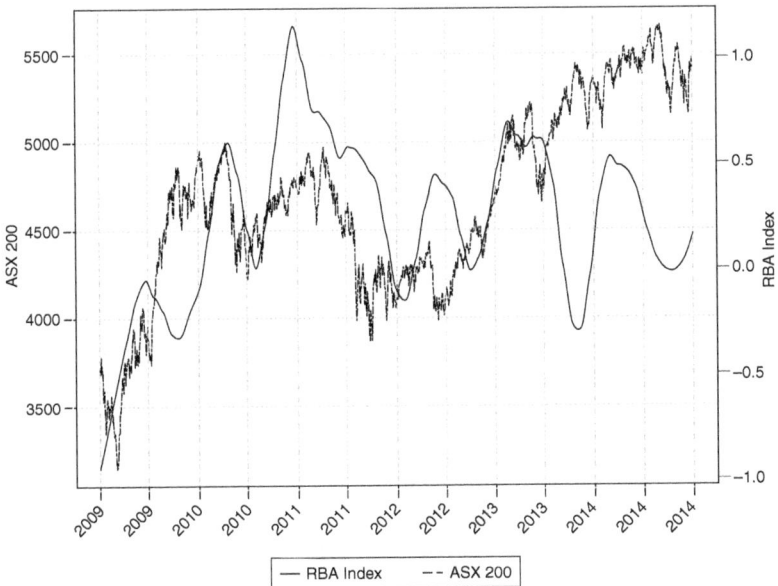

Figure 14.1 RBA Index, the ASX 500, and SSE Composite Index.

hawkishness seems out of place. If exports to China are so vital to the Australian economy, then this hawkish position would seem to run contrary to that end: hawkish policy, after all, is essentially contractionary and leads to disinflationary pressure, and, for countries strongly reliant on foreign demand for commodities, a weak currency is vital for economic growth. That being the case, why did the RBA trend hawkish? The immediate answer to that question lies in the scale of this trend. While the RBA did trend hawkish from 2010 to 2015, the upward limit of this hawkishness is positive 0.5. Whether hawkish or dovish, any score that falls so close to zero is actually closer to neutral than anything else, and, with that taken into account, the hawkish fluctuations can be understood better as subtle modulations—perhaps even small moves to keep in line with another trend. Given the Australian economy's relationship with the Chinese market, it would seem plausible that these small movements could be connected to an effort to maintain that delicate balance.

* * *

While the recent, relatively granular fluctuations in the RBA Index may point toward a China-centric communication policy, its points of divergence with the Australian economy may also be rooted in this connection. For example, definitive points of divergence are seen in Figure 14.2, which compares RBA Index trends to the Australian fixed-income market.

The RBA Index, represented by the solid black line, often exhibits a predictive relationship with the ten-year bond yield, represented by the broken line. For instance, from the middle of 2010 to the middle of 2012 the RBA Index and the ten-year bond share similar paths—with the ten-year bond reflecting RBA market sentiments within three to four months—and this period of predictive movement is bookended by similarly connected trends in both data streams.

But could trends in RBA communications have bearing outside the Australian economy? The answer to this question lies in the relationship between Australia and China that has been central to this chapter: perhaps, along with the Australian economy, the RBA is reacting to the China. When the RBA Index is compared to the Chinese stock market—instead of Australian equities—this hypothesis seems to be borne out by the facts in Figure 14.3.

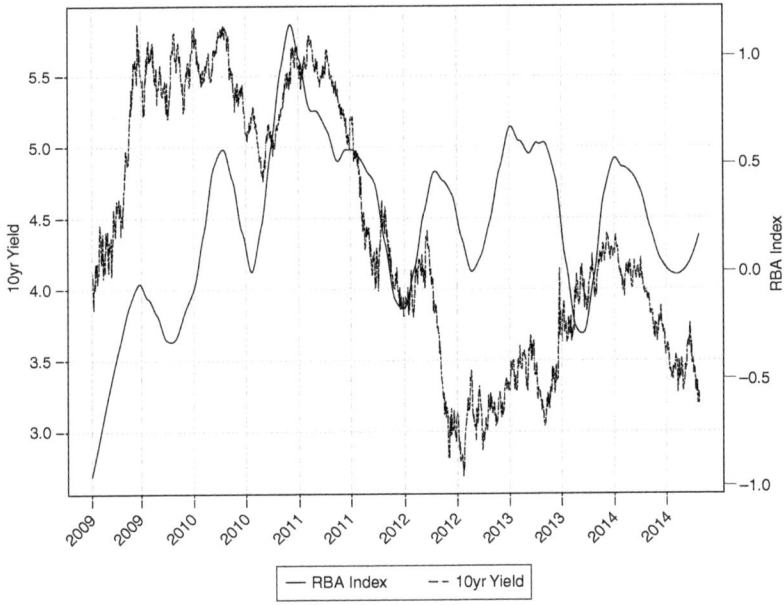

Figure 14.2 RBA Index and Australian government ten-year bond yield.

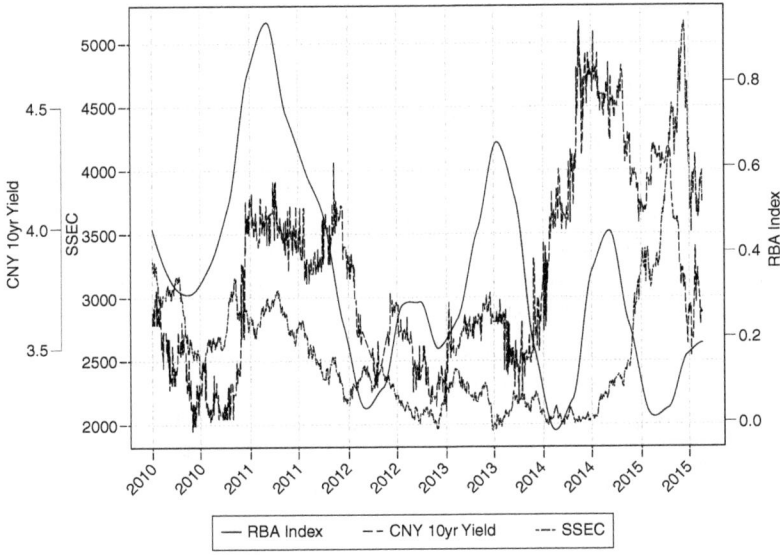

Figure 14.3 RBA Index and Chinese benchmarks.

The Shanghai Stock Exchange Composite (SSEC) is depicted in Figure 14.3 by the broken and dotted line and the RBA Index by the solid line. Figure 14.3 suggests that the RBA Index shares a very strong—seemingly prescient—relationship with the performance of the Chinese stock market, as the peaks and valleys of the central bank's mood are soon mirrored in the market's fluctuations. This dynamic can be seen throughout the five-year span chronicled by the figure. In early 2010, when the SSEC is still on a downward trend, the RBA Index starts to rise sharply, and this ascent is manifested nearly six months later in the SSEC. The RBA Index then peaks and begins to dive from early 2011 to early 2012 and, over the same time period, the Chinese stock market experiences the same movements—albeit a few months after the RBA Index. From the beginning of 2012 to the end of 2014, the RBA Index climbs to a peak in the summer of 2012, dives off from then to late 2012, then peaks again in mid-2013 and descends until early 2014. Once again, the SSEC reflects these changes (with less drama) a few months later: from late-2012 to spring 2013, the market climbs to a peak; after this the SSEC descends—only to peak again later in 2013 and descend once more until 2014.

Along with its relationship to the Chinese stock market, the RBA Index also can serve as a leading indicator (0.245 correlation) for the Chinese bond yields (represented in Figure 14.3 by the broken line). This is particularly evident from the middle of 2010 until the beginning of 2011, where the bond yield's jumps are anticipated by the upward trending RBA sentiment. When not clearly leading, RBA Index movements still correlate closely with the Chinese fixed income. The RBA Index trends from early 2012 to early 2014 track closely with income fluctuations—a dynamic that is clearly noticeable in the RBA Index peak that occurs in mid-2014 and 2015 and mid-2014 and 2015's bold yield peaks.

In both the Chinese fixed-income and equity market benchmarks, every substantial market movement is either correlated—or anticipated and correlated—by the movements of the RBA Index. This data presents an interesting—and perhaps foreseeable—conclusion: the RBA's communications seem strongly influenced by the projected performance of the Chinese economy and, therefore, the RBA's mood may be leading indicator of the Chinese market fluctuations and the Australian economy. This, of course, strongly supports the use of the RBA—specifically the sentiment of RBA texts—as a window into Chinese economic activity.

This technique is further justified when currency trends presented in Figure 14.4 are examined.

The RBA Index, the solid black line, and the Australian dollar-Chinese yuan, the broken and dotted line, share similar fluctuations from 2003 to 2009, but, from 2009 onward, their movements are extremely tight. The RBA Index breaks out of the 2008 crisis in early 2009, pulling itself from negative 1 on the Index scale to neutral over the course of less than a year. The AUD-CNY moves with the central bank's sentiment, beginning its own upward climb just months afterward. In 2011, they both hit their highs—with the RBA Index leading—as the RBA Index approached positive 1 and AUD-CNY just exceeding a 7-to-1 exchange rate. The ensuing downturn and ascent in the RBA Index are, once again, in concert with market movements.

Interestingly, if a less-smoothed average of the RBA Index is employed—allowing the sentiment be more powerfully swayed by

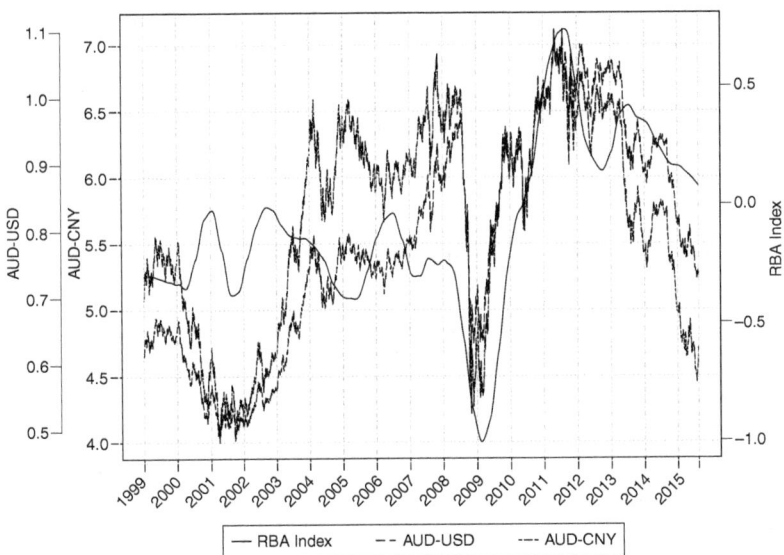

Figure 14.4 AUD-CNY and RBA Index.

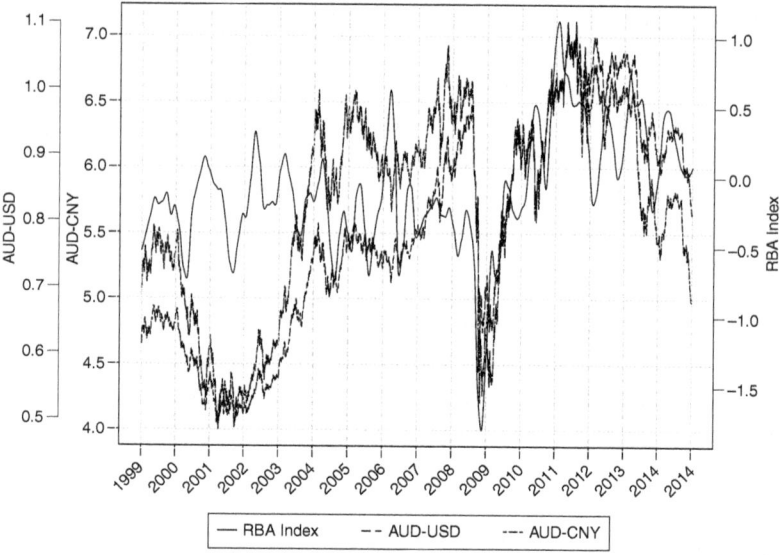

Figure 14.5 AUD-CNY and RBA Index (less smoothed).

the day-to-day positions of central bankers—then an even tighter dynamic emerges, which is presented in Figure 14.5.

From 2004 on, the RBA Index and the AUD-CNY movements are closely linked—an 11-year stretch of correlation that is yet another indicator that a strong relationship exists between the outlook of the RBA and Chinese economy.

* * *

Beyond further bolstering this thesis, the accuracy provided by the less smoothed average highlights an advantage of the data we've created through a systematic analysis of central banking communications: its versatility. Through a historical analysis of market and central bank communication trends, the transformation of the sentiment data that seems most suited to the specific market under scrutiny can be found. This is not a case of ad hoc alignment, but instead an examination of how central banking moods proliferate into the diverse financial mechanisms that drive economy. Some markets, by the nature of the financial instruments they concern, will inherently be more responsive to the day-to-day attitude of a central banking. The FOREX market is a perfect example of this kind of sensitivity, as economic trends are quickly digested and acted upon through the agile trading strategies that drive currency exchange. The markets that seem to better align with general index trends, like commodities markets, are likely those markets whose movements are more generated by the slower hand of monetary policy and broad communication themes.

* * *

Australia is certainly home to a major economy in its own right, and that importance is only magnified when its ties to the Chinese market are explored. The compelling patterns that our data has identified suggest that a deeper investigation of these connections—particularly leveraging RBA texts—could help lift the veil of opacity that surrounds the second largest (possibly the largest) economy in the world. Embedded with multitiered significance, RBA communications represent a truly rich macroeconomic indicator, capturing the complex interplay at work among the RBA, the Australian, and the Chinese economies. For financial professionals looking to understand the RBA, either of these economies, or all of the above, the RBA Index could serve as an innovative and important part of that process.

This additional insight could be particularly helpful given the slowdown in growth that China has been experiencing in recent years:

> Structurally, China's economy faces headwinds. In the long run, growth is a function of changes in labour, capital and productivity. When all three increase, as they did in China for many years, growth rates are superlative. But they are all slowing now. China's working-age population peaked in 2012. Investment also looks to have topped out (at 49% of GDP, a level few countries have ever seen). Finally, China's technological gap with rich countries is narrower than in the past, implying that productivity growth will be lower, too. (The Economist 2015)

As China grapples with uncertain economic conditions while it continues to preserve secrecy within its central bank, it will become increasingly important for market players to leverage what data streams they have at their disposal to make informed decisions in a difficult environment. From what our data demonstrates, RBA communications appear to be a vital resource toward that end.

15

Global Sentiment: International Central Bank Transparency

The Federal Reserve. The European Central Bank. The Bank of England. The Bank of Japan. The Reserve Bank of Australia. The People's Bank of China. Exploring their history, politics, and processes, this book has tackled this influential group to assess the development of transparency within central banking's most significant institutions. This is not to diminish the power of other central banks. All central banks have tremendous economic sway—if not globally, domestically—and consequently merit the attention of those who wish to have a grasp on the financial world. In light of this necessity, this chapter picks up where the last four left off, concisely cataloguing the background and current strategies of a host of additional institutions. This chapter does not cover every central bank in the world; there are over a hundred. Instead, we review a selection of institutions that represent the three general categories that central banks fall into globally: banks in developed countries that are transparent, banks in developed countries that have yet to firmly embrace transparency, and, banks, regardless of transparency, of emerging national economies. An integral element of this account will be our sentiment data and the bearing it has on each of the economies these banks preside over. By taking this approach, this chapter aims to afford both a better understanding of central banking operations worldwide and the broad applications of our methodology, expanding on the global perspective that was afforded by the earlier chapter on central banks and currency trading.

* * *

Transparent Banks of Developed Economies

Bank of Canada

The Bank of Canada (BOC) is one of the most transparent banks in the world. The BOC was founded as a privately owned institution in March 1935 as a reaction to the Great Depression and the resulting worldwide economic plunge. In 1938, the bank, headquartered in Ottawa, was nationalized under a mandate "to regulate currency in the best interests of the economic life of the nation" (Bank of Canada 2015b). Today, the mission of the bank remains "to promote the economic and financial welfare of Canada" with four core functions: establishing the monetary policy, maintaining the financial system, issuing currency, and overseeing funds management (Bank of Canada 2015a). The goal of the current monetary policy is to preserve the value of the Canadian dollar by keeping inflation predictable, low, and stable.

In order to accomplish this objective, the BOC has set an inflation-control target of 2 percent, the midpoint of its 1- to 3-percent acceptable range. The target was set in 1991 and is reviewed every five years. Additionally, Canada's flexible exchange rate allows the bank to adopt an independent monetary policy that is the most beneficial in Canada's economic climate and most useful for attaining the inflation target. The bank has also recently made efforts to increase transparency, including launching the operating band for the overnight interest rate, publicizing forecasts about the economy in the semi-annual Monetary Policy Report, setting eight fixed announcement dates throughout the year to note the inflation-control target rate setting, and issuing press releases to explain the rationale behind policy changes.

The BOC offers Maple Bonds, which are "Canadian-dollar-denominated bonds issued by foreign borrowers in the domestic Canadian fixed-income market," domestic Government of Canada bonds, and saving bonds (Hately 2012).

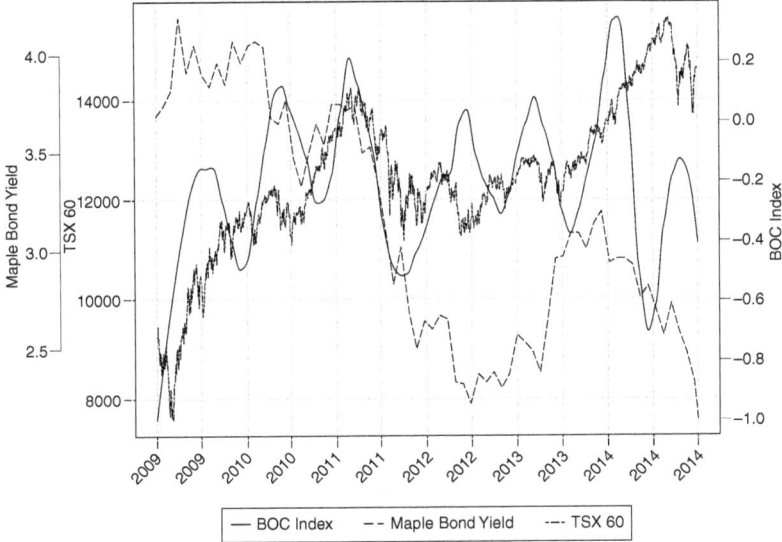

Figure 15.1 BOC Index and TSX 60.

An analysis of Figure 15.1 suggests that our data serves as a useful indicator for the Canadian Security Exchange's TSX 60.

Figure 15.1 presents the TSX 60's index along with the Band of Canada Index (BOC Index). The TSX 60 is represented by the broken and dotted line, while the BOC Index is represented by the solid black line. The BOC Index's general trend from very dovish to neutral, along with variance in the data, anticipates, mirrors, then anticipates the variance in the increase in equities prices. From early 2009 to early 2011, the BOC Index leads the TSX 60 with its fluctuations, trending toward positive gains. This two-year stretch is followed by three years—spring 2011 through spring 2014—of back and forth leading and following. Finally, from early 2014 on, the BOC Index regains its lead on the market: the valley, followed by a peak and an ensuing valley are all ahead of the index movements. This suggests that the BOC Index is useful as both a leading indicator for equity market developments and as a market barometer.

Bank of Sweden (Riksbank)

The Bank of Sweden, or the Riksbank, is not only considered the world's oldest bank, it's also believed to be the most transparent

(Holmes 2013). Although it has been around since 1667, the Riksbank did not become the official central bank of Sweden until the 1897 Riksbank Act. Located in Stockholm, the Riksbank operates under the Swedish parliament. Today, the Riksbank's main objective is to "maintain price stability" by sustaining a low, secure rate of inflation (Sveriges Riksbank 2015b). The 2 percent inflation target was applied in 1995 and has remained at that point ever since.

The Riksbank is led by an Executive Board of six members, made up of a governor and five deputy governors. Members of the Executive Board are appointed for a period of five or six years by the bank's General Council, which in turn is appointed by the Swedish parliament. General Council members do not have the right to vote on or propose policies to the Executive Board. The governor is selected from the members of the board, also by the General Council. The Executive Board holds six meetings a year to discuss its monetary policy and changes to the bank rate. In order to promote greater transparency, the Riksbank publishes press releases after each meeting as well as a Monetary Policy Report that contains forecasts for inflation and economic changes (Sveriges Riksbank 2015a).

The Riksbank offers government bonds through the Swedish National Debt Office. Their maturation timelines range from two to ten years. Swedish equities are traded on the Stockholm Stock Exchange, known as OMX. Its major indexes include OMX S30 and the OMX Nordic 40, which represent baskets of top equities.

Figures 15.2 and 15.3 set our data alongside the benchmark data for the Swedish equities (OMX 30) and fixed income markets (ten-year government bond), demonstrating its use as an indicator for both markets. Figure 15.2 presents the Bank of Sweden Index (SWE Index) alongside the OMX 30 index.

The broken line represents the OMX 30, and the solid black line represents the SWE Index. The general trends in the index and the central bank's mood appear to be inversely related. As the sentiment indicator drops from very hawkish (1.6) to moderately hawkish (0.8) from January of 2009 to January of 2012, the equities index sees a general ascent. This trend continues as the sentiment indicator drops to almost neutral. As general movements in the SWE

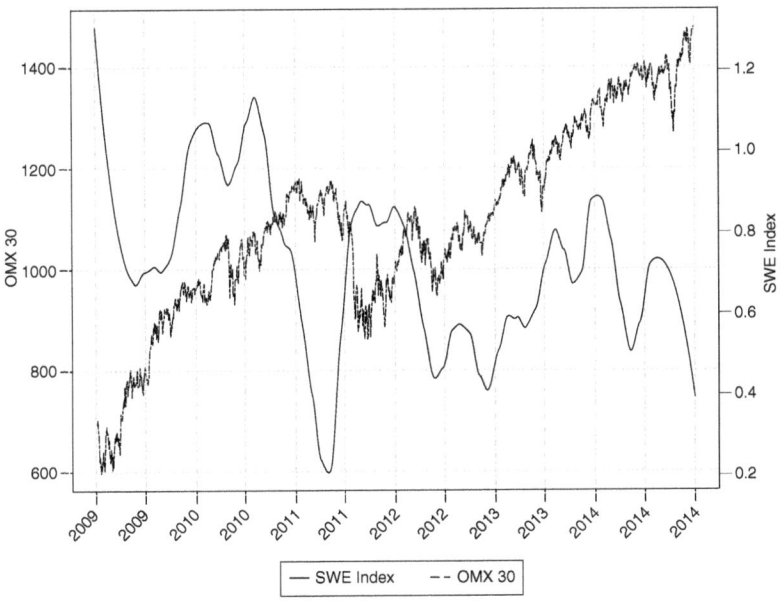

Figure 15.2 SWE Index and OMX 30.

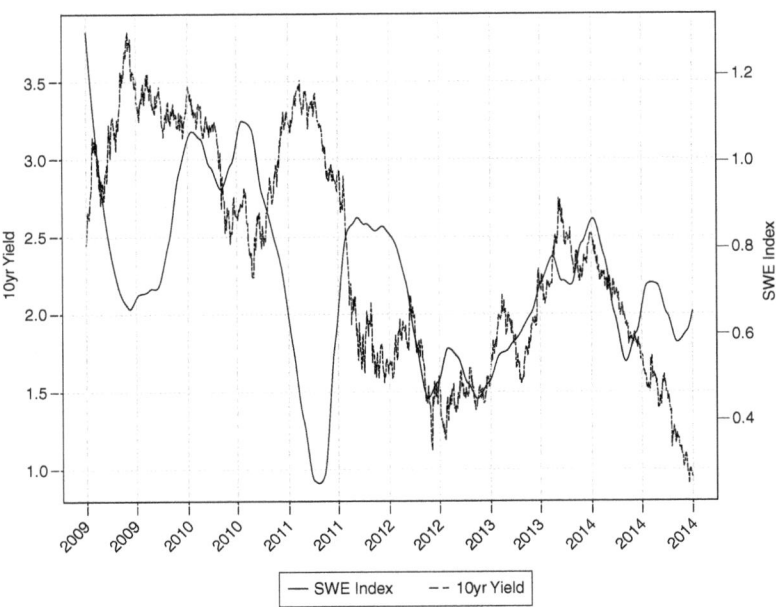

Figure 15.3 SWE Index and Swedish government ten-year bond yield.

Index seem connected to market gains and losses (often anticipating them), this inverse relationship could be used by financial professionals to understand (and predict) market conditions.

Figure 15.3 presents the sentiment indicator alongside the Swedish government's ten-year bond yield.

The solid black line represents the sentiment indicator, while the broken line represents the ten-year bond yield. Movements in the sentiment indicator are exaggerated in the bond yield, and, as it was with the equities, the SWE Index is split between reflecting and anticipating the bond yield. From 20010 to late 2012, the sentiment indicator leads the ten-year bond yield by a period of five to seven months. In the winter of 2012, this leading becomes tracking, as the both the SWE Index and the bond yield rise and fall in unison.

Reserve Bank of New Zealand

The Reserve Bank of New Zealand (RBNZ) was founded in 1934 in Wellington. Although the government was initially reluctant, the Great Depression and pressing foreign economic issues made the need for a central bank clear, and over the last 80 years the RBNZ has become one of the most transparent banks on earth. Upon its creation, the reserve bank's policies were aimed at enhancing growth, reducing unemployment, and keeping prices stable. Today, the reserve bank's uses monetary policy to contain inflation by keeping it within a targeted range. In 1989, Government of New Zealand gave the reserve bank the statutory authority to control inflation. It does this by updating its Policy Targets Agreement (PTA) between the governor of the reserve bank and the Minister of Finance to agree to keep inflation between 1 and 3 percent a year on average. Additionally, since March 1999, the reserve bank has implemented the Official Cash Rate (OCR), an interest rate set by the bank to meet the inflation band previously specified. The OCR is reviewed eight times a year. Over the last several decades, the RBNZ has made a concerted effort to build upon its tradition of open communication by embracing increasing transparency measures (Reserve Bank of New Zealand 2015).

The utility of Prattle's data for New Zealand assets is exemplified in its application to interpreting currency fluctuations. Figure 15.4 sets the RNZ Index (thin black line) beside the New Zealand dollar-basket of currencies pair (thick black line).

As Figure 15.4 illustrates, there is a strong correlation between the RNZ Index and the currency movements. Throughout the timeframe captured, the RNZ Index shifts between correlating with the currency fluctuation and correlating and anticipating the movements. From January of 2005 until the same month in 2009, the RNZ clearly anticipates every major currency fluctuation, powerfully dipping and driving eight to six months before the market reflects these trends. From early 2009 to mid-2010, the dynamic reverses—with the RNZ Index trailing the currency movements. Then the RNZ Index retains its trend-leading status, anticipating the market dip of mid-2010–early 2011 with its own rapid downward trend. From 2011 to 2014, the RNZ Index's fluctuations become noticeably more reserved than the currency's, but the central banks mood still shows predictive stretches—the late 2012/early 2013 RNZ Index dip serves as a leading indicator for mid-2013's currency drop. With this comparison in mind, it seems

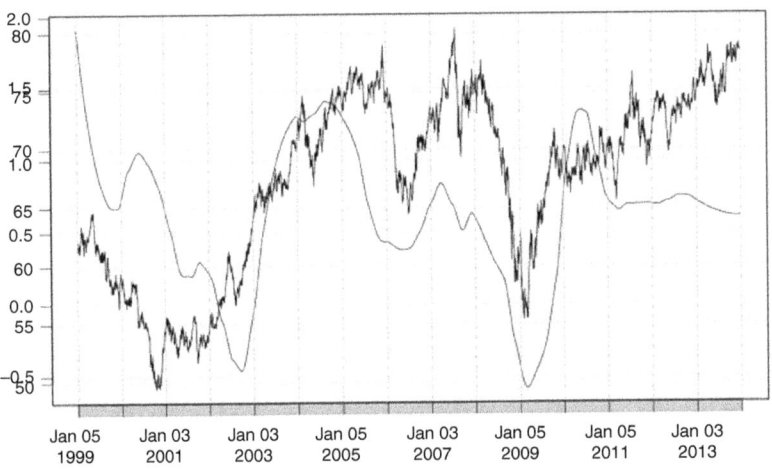

Figure 15.4 RNZ Index and exchange rates.

clear that the RNZ Index shares an identifiable relationship with the currency market.

* * *

(Slightly) Less Transparent Banks of Developed Economies

Swiss National Bank

The Schweizerische Nationalbank, also known as the Swiss National Bank (SNB), was founded by Federal Act in 1907 to insure price stability and provide informed management of Swiss economic developments. Established as a special statute joint-stock company, it is administered under the supervision of the Swiss Confederation, which—unlike most national banks—does not own a single share of the bank. Instead, the bank's 25-million-franc capital is split roughly 55–45 among public shareholders, the Swiss cantons, and cantonal banks and private investors. The reason for the central bank's distributed ownership, specifically among the cantonal banks, is the federated nature of the Swiss government. The bank is governed by general meetings of shareholders, which occur once per year. In the interim, bank operations are managed by the Governing Board, Enlarged Governing Board, and the eleven-member Bank Council; five of whom are elected by the Shareholders' Meeting and six of whom are elected by the Federal Government (Swiss National Bank 2015).

The SNB defines price stability as less than 2 percent inflation per year—but, unlike other central banks, this mark represents an upper bound instead of a target. Given the power to set interest rates on its deposit accounts and control the cash supply, the SNB implements its monetary policy by manipulating the levers it has been given. The SNB executes its policy from its two head offices, located in Zurich and Bern, along with six representative offices peppered throughout the country, and fourteen agencies operated by cantonal banks. Perhaps the bank's most significant achievement is its maintenance of the franc: since the SNB's founding in 1907, the Swiss franc has well outperformed all other currencies, losing only 87 percent of its value vis-à-vis gold over the past century while most other currencies have lost roughly 99 percent. Since the onset of the financial crisis, the SNB has battled Switzerland's low inflation rate by experimenting with pegging and de-pegging from the euro (Swiss National Bank 2015).

Figure 15.5 presents the Swiss National Bank Index (SNB Index), represented by the broken black line, alongside the Swiss Market Index (SMI), which is represented by the solid black line. Since 2009, the SNB's communications have been generally dovish with a trend toward hawkishness, with the exception of a hawkish spike in mid-2011. This suggests that the SNB's policy has been to encourage inflation even as disinflation concerns slowly eased; indeed, as the discussion above highlights, the SNB has adamantly fought against Switzerland's low inflation rate, only recently curbing its measures. Similarly, the hawkish spike in mid-2011 is not out of the ordinary when considering the context: Switzerland faced major doubts about its financial strength after its foreign exchange reserves were depleted—a consequence of the recession (Jordan 2011). The SNB had to react to decreasing confidence in the equities market with hawkish policy—which ultimately resulted in the bank abandoning its peg to the euro. Their actions and the market's subsequent

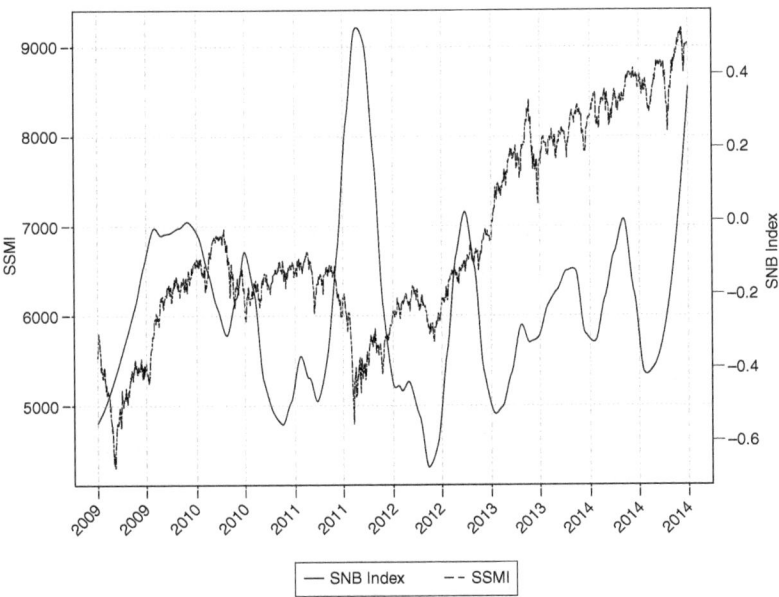

Figure 15.5 SNB Index and Swiss Market Index (SMI).

adjustment are echoed in the figure. One can see how the story told by the data is corroborated once the events that took place are considered.

When compared with the SMI, the SNB Index serves as a leading indicator. A general peak and subsequent denouement in mid-2009 to mid-2011 serve as precursors to similar movements in the equities index. After the hawkish spike, which was in reaction to concerns about the strength of the franc, we see that the SMI rallies—in other words, the corrective actions (such as pegging to the euro) taken by the SNB boosted confidence in the market. Several Index fluctuations in the dovish direction along the way, like those in early 2012 and mid-2014, lead small market adjustments roughly four to six months following. In light of the correlated trends and the strong mechanistic connection the contextual analysis suggests, the data could prove useful to those interested in examining the relationship between the Swedish equities market and the Swedish National Bank's sentiment. Our data could also benefit FOREX market players, as the Swiss franc is one of the most heavily traded currencies in the world—and thus demonstrating the value of any additional insight into the actions and attitude of the SNB.

Bank of Korea

The Bank of Korea (BOK) was founded on June 12, 1950 through the Bank of Korea Act. The bank is located in Seoul. It was founded to insure price stability and to maintain inflation at certain rates to maximize economic output and employment (Bank of Korea 2015). Like other central banks, the BOK's other functions include issuing banknotes and coins, supervising financial institutions, and managing South Korea's foreign reserves.

The traditional policy of the bank has followed closely what its Western counterparts have done. Manipulation of interest rates has been stable and predictable, and the bank has largely maintained independence from government pressure. In the wake of the 2008 financial crisis, the bank has become more responsive to government demands and has cut interest rates to historic lows (1.75 percent) (Kim and Yoo 2014) and has missed its target rate of inflation (Mundy and Jung-a 2015). The BOK engages in open market operations in order to control inflation and preserve the purchasing power of the won.

The BOK is transparent with regards to the frequency of its communications, but is less so when comes to the quality of the information they release. As of 2015, rate-setting meetings occur every month, and the bank publishes minutes following these meetings. There are proposals being considered to move toward less frequent meetings that yield more substantive communications.

As with a number of other central banks, the utility of our data is evidenced by its predictive relationship to the Korean Stock Exchange 100 (KRX 100). Figure 15.6 presents the KRX 100 index along with the Bank of Korea Index (BOK Index).

The KRX 100 index is represented by the broken line, while the BOK Index is represented by the solid black line. Clearly, the KRX 100 is a very volatile index, with several peaks and troughs coupled with cyclic, pronounced variance. Yet, remarkably, the BOK Index's tune is on key: peaks and troughs in the BOK Index lead peaks and troughs in the KRX 100 by two to four months. This suggests that the BOK Index is a strong leading indicator for Korean equity activity.

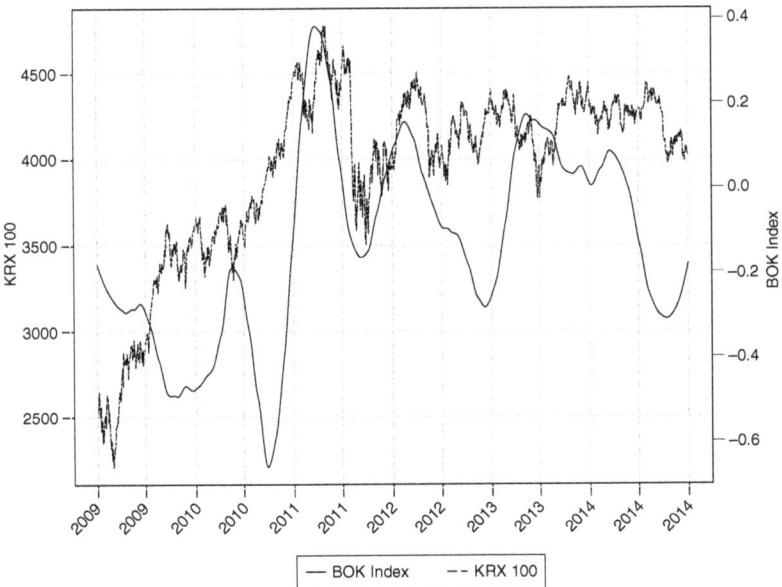

Figure 15.6 BOK Index and KRX 100.

Bank of Israel

The Bank of Israel (BOI) was established on August 24, 1954 through the Bank of Israel Act. The bank's mandate is to maintain price stability, preserve the purchasing power of the shekel, support government economic policy, and to maintain the stability of the Israeli financial system (Bank of Israel 2015).

The traditional policy of the bank has been fairly conservative. Israeli development occurred rapidly after statehood, benefiting from large capital inflows. This meant that the bank had to do little to spur economic development and growth—but had to double-down on inflationary pressure. Policy is aimed at maintaining the competitiveness of the shekel so Israeli goods are attractive on export markets, and, to this end, the bank has set the target inflation rate in a range from 1 to 3 percent. The low or negative inflation in post-financial-crisis years has, however, resulted in interest rates near 0.0 percent.

Although fairly transparent, the BOI is less transparent than several of its counterparts in other developed countries; the BOI publishes information and reports less frequently, their reporting is of a lower quality and contain less information, and the bank's policy is mandated to support government policy, reducing the bank's independence relative to Western central banks (Nissan 2015). The bank's five-member monetary policy panel makes decisions regarding monetary policy. This concentration of decision-making power in a smaller group further contributes to reduced transparency.

The predictive capacity of our data on the Israeli central bank is demonstrated below in a comparison to the government's ten-year bond yield. Figure 15.7 presents the BOI Index vis-à-vis the Israeli government ten-year bond yield.

The ten-year bond is represented by the broken line, while the BOI Index is represented by the solid black line. The BOI Index's peaks and troughs consistently predate changes in the bond yield by roughly six months, suggesting that the BOI Index is a leading indicator of bond movements. The decline seen in the bond yield from mid-2009 to late 2010 is prefigured in the BOI Index trends, as is late 2010 and early 2011's yield surge. The sentiment indicator once again leads the strong, general declines seen from then on with its own intense descent, predicting a slight upward trend with

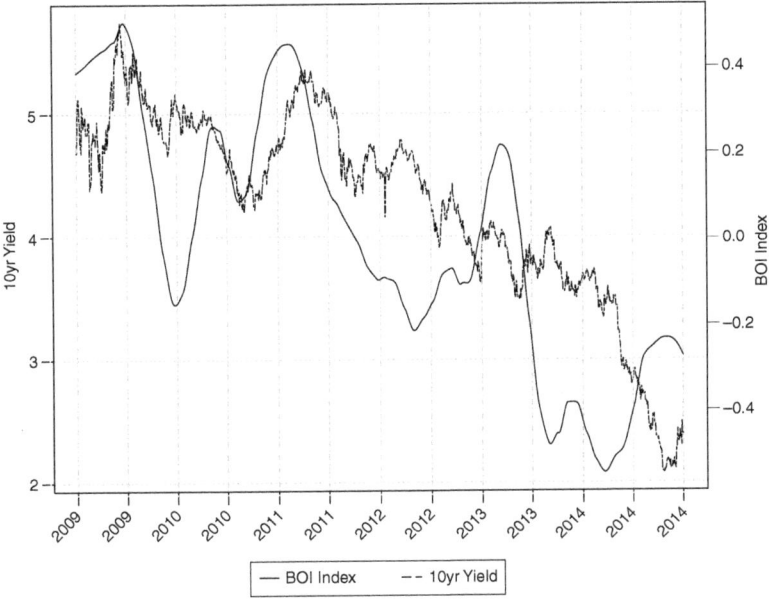

Figure 15.7 BOI Index and Israeli government ten-year bond yield.

an exaggerated flourish. In short, the BOI Index proves to be a useful leading indicator of this benchmark fixed income rate.

Bank of Mexico

The Bank of Mexico (BOM) was founded on September 1, 1925, after revolution fractured the ability of the retail banks to issue reliable and trustworthy bank notes. In July 1931, the Monetary Law was passed, establishing the peso as the official currency, as a demonetization of gold, and formalizing the bank's power. Its duties since have been to print currency, preserve the purchasing power of the peso, and make sure inflation creates conditions ripe for sustained growth and job creation. The bank is located in the Federal District of Mexico City (Bank of Mexico 2015a).

In the spirit of an open market of retail bank competition, the BOM was established by government funds as an autonomous institution. The bank buys and sells reserves and securities on the open market. The bank is managed by a board of governors made up of five officials—a governor and four deputies—appointed by the president and confirmed by the senate. The governor is appointed for a six-year term, while the deputy governors are appointed for eight-year terms. The current governor is Agustín Carstens (Bank of Mexico 2015b).

The BOM takes government reporting and oversight seriously and, consequently, has begun to take meaningful steps toward transparency. In fact, board members and central bank staff are subject to the Federal Civil Servants Liability Law, which allows for their impeachment if they are not meeting the standards set by the bank. The bank reports its policies and activities to Congress and their publishing schedule is public knowledge. Reports are published frequently.

Since 1996, the bank has set annual inflation targets. As of 2015, the target is set at 3 percent per year. Similarly, the bank rate, like the federal funds rate, is set at 3 percent per year. The Government of Mexico offers bonds ranging in maturity from overnight to 30 years. Equities are traded on the Mexican Stock Exchange, located in Mexico City's financial district. The exchanges primary index is the Indice de Precios y Cotizaciones (IPC).

Comparing our data on the to the Mexican Stock Exchange's IPC, Figure 15.8 presents the IPC's index along with the Bank of Mexico Index (BOM Index).

The broken line represents the IPC, while the solid black line represents the BOM Index. The BOM Index's undulating movement from neutral dovish to moderately hawkish during the 2009–2012 time period accurately predates symmetrical movements by the IPC by about six months. The BOM Index's fluctuations are, however, far more extreme than their equity counterparts, and this exaggerated dynamic is seen most clearly from the end of the 2013 to the beginning of 2014, where a relatively minor market dip is prefigured by an enormous sentiment indicator plunge. This fluctuation indicates that the BOM is extremely sensitive to market conditions and likely a very reliable indicator of even minor market changes.

* * *

Banks of Emerging Economies

The terms BRICS has become common among those involved in international finance. While originally referencing Brazil, Russia,

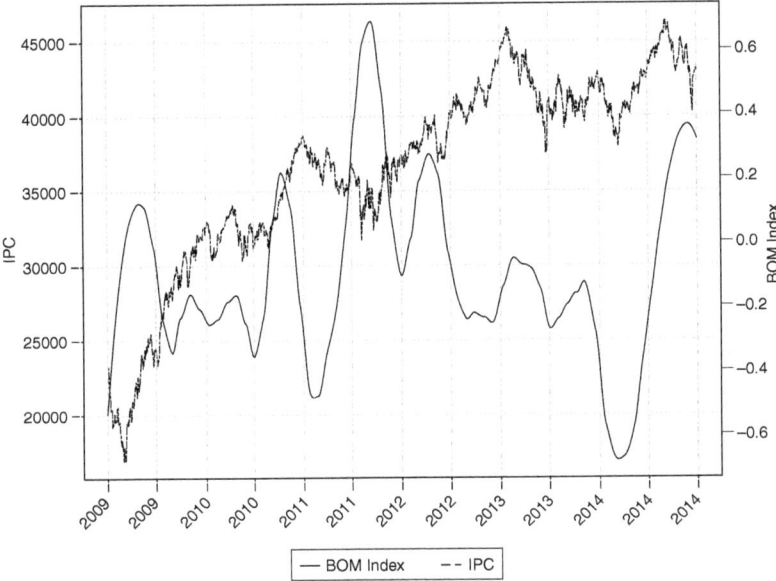

Figure 15.8 BOM Index and Mexican IPC.

India, China, and South Africa, the acronym has now become synonymous with systemically important, rapidly growing developing economies. Because of data limitations we've already discussed, the PBoC was already touched on in an earlier chapter. This section will focus on Brazil, Russia, India, and South Africa.

Central Bank of Brazil

The Central Bank of Brazil (BCB) as we know it today arose from the centuries-separated marriage of the Brazilian Mint (established in 1694), the Bank of Brazil (established in 1808 by John VI of Portugal), and the Superintendency for the Currency and Credit (SUMOC) (established by decree of President Vargas in 1945). The central bank—formally opened in December of 1964—came into being 270 years after its metaphorical cornerstone had been laid. The bank's operation, however, did not begin peacefully: the Central Bank of Brazil began negotiating its status as Brazil's single monetary authority in the aftermath of the 1964 Brazilian coup d'état, which established Brazil's military government. When considering the bank's precarious birth, the levels of accountability and monetary efficacy it has achieved are remarkable (Central Bank of Brazil 2015a).

Today, the bank is headquartered in Brasília. The CBB's complex policymaking structure is overseen by a board of governors. This board is comprised of a governor and the deputy governors for each of the bank's secretariats. The bank's monetary policy, though, is determined by the bank's Monetary Policy Committee, also referred to as COPOM. With the power to set monetary policy and the short-term interest rate, known as the SELIC rate, COPOM is responsible for the protection of the Brazilian real. COPOM is composed of the members of the board of governors, including the governor and the several deputy governors for Monetary Policy, Economic Policy, International Affairs and Risk Management, Financial Regulation, Financial System Organization, Control of Farm Credit, Supervision, Administration, Institutional Relations and Citizenship (Central Bank of Brazil 2015b).

The SELIC rate, as of 2015, is set at 13.25 percent, the highest it has been since January of 2009, a 6 percent increase from the 2013's low of 7.25 percent. This high bank rate is a side effect of lowered growth expectations for the country's slowing economy, which place estimates for 2015 growth around 1.8 percent, and raise inflation expectations, which are estimated to be around 6 percent in 2015. Brazilian equities are traded on the BM&F BOVESPA stock exchange.

To illustrate how our data measures up as a tool for understanding the Brazilian market, Figure 15.9 places the Brazilian Central Bank Index (BCB Index) beside the BOVESPA.

The BCB Index is represented by the solid black line and the broken line represents the BOVESPA Index. While exaggerated, the movements in the BCB Index consistently prefigure equity movements. In mid-2013, while the market is still generally trending downward, the BCB Index is making gains, climbing until autumn before falling until the end of the year. An analogous trend is seen in a few months later in equities. From spring 2014 until summer 2014, equities again leap up—an upward trend that is anticipated in the Index movements of that year. The BCB Index then rapidly dives—mid-2014 through late 2014—and the market follows suit—late summer through the very end of the year. The BCB Index

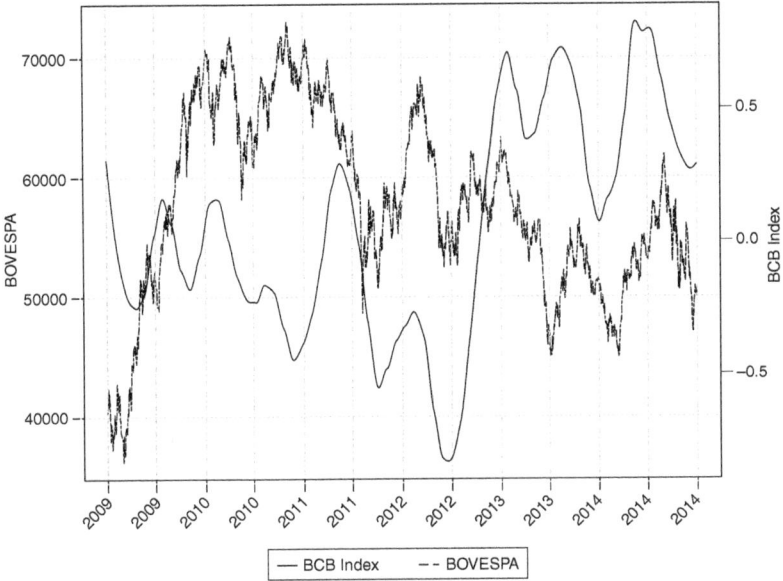

Figure 15.9 BCB Index and the BM&F BOVESPA Index.

continues to anticipate or reflect changes in the equity market for the rest of the timeline. Given the correspondence between the two data streams, a relationship between the Brazilian Central Bank's communications and the Brazilian equities market seems apparent.

Bank of Russia

Like most central banks, The Bank of Russia's mission is to insure the stability of Russia's national currency, the ruble, through monetary policy. Unlike most central banks, however, the Bank of Russia—or, as it is formally named, the Central Bank of the Russian Federation—was founded a mere 25 years ago on July 13, 1990, as one of the last wishes of the dying USSR. Its recent founding makes it one of youngest central banks in the world. Accountable to the Supreme Soviet of the RSFSR, it was originally called the State Bank of the RSFSR. The bank's mission is to protect the nation's currency through the levers of monetary policy persists today. Further, the bank notes that though "it is not a body of state power, [...] its powers are, in effect, the functions of a body of state power, because their implementation implies the use of state compulsion" (Bank of Russia 2015c). In this sense, the bank carries the power of the Russian government with it—and thus, so do its communications.

Though it is independently managed on a day-to-day basis, the Bank of Russia is wholly owned by the Russian government, answerable to the State Duma of the Federal Assembly. The bank is governed by a board of governors. The State Duma appoints and dismisses the board's governor when prompted to do so by the president of the Russian Federation. The appointed governor, in turn, nominates the appointment and dismissal of members for the board, which are officially appointed or dismissed by the State Duma in agreement with the president of the Russian Federation (Bank of Russia 2015b).

As Russia's 2014–2015 gross domestic product (GDP) growth forecast hovered at 3.3 percent, the Bank of Russia decided to alter their planned 4 percent inflation target, instead raising it to 5 percent. As of May 2015, the key rate—much like the federal funds rate—was set at 12.5 percent (Bank of Russia 2015a).

How does our data stack up to the Russian equity markets? Figure 15.10 allows for an easy comparison between the Central Bank of Russia Index (CBR Index) and the MICEX.

Late 2012 through mid-2014, the CBR Index, the solid black line, and the MICEX, the broken line, share common fluctuations. The CBR Index's peaks and valleys generally prefigure several market movements. This connection only intensifies after the summer of 2014: the ensuing dive and rapid climb seen in the CBR Index reflect market conditions. This suggests that correlation between the central banks communicative arm and the economy is only on the rise. The data gives Russian central bank watchers cause for optimism, as it appears that CBR communication will continue to be a significant force in the market—and therefore represents a dependable financial data resource.

Reserve Bank of India

The Reserve Bank of India (RBI) was founded on April 1, 1935 by virtue of the Reserve Bank of India Act. The Bank of India was

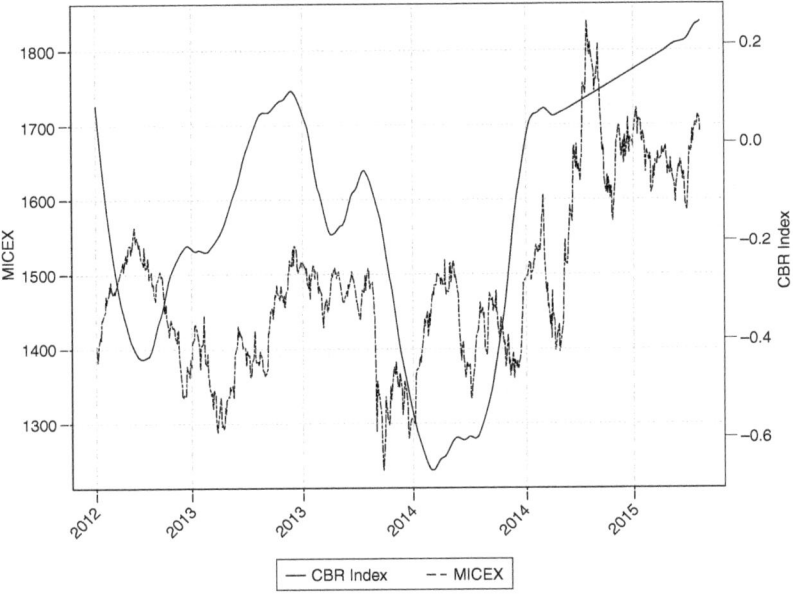

Figure 15.10 CBR Index and the MICEX Index.

established to "regulate the issue of Bank Notes," insure "monetary stability in India," and generally to "operate the currency and credit system of the country to its advantage" (Reserve Bank of India 2015b). Though originally privately owned, the bank was nationalized in 1949 and is now fully owned by the Government of India. The bank is currently headquartered in Mumbai.

Like most central banks, the RBI is governed by a central board of directors. The board consists of a governor, four deputy governors, and fourteen directors. All officers are appointed for terms of four years by the Government of India; four of the directors must come from local bank boards in Mumbai, Calcutta, Chennai, and New Delhi, and one director must be a government official (Reserve Bank of India 2015a).

The inflation rate in India has varied between 12.0 and 6.4 percent per year since 2010. In 2015, the RBI set an inflation target of below 6 percent per year by January 2016 and a 4 percent per year target following that. Since 2015, the RBI's bank rate—similar to the federal funds rate—rests at 8.75 percent per year (Reserve Bank of India 2015b).

Indian equities are traded on the Bombay Stock Exchange (BSE). The S&P BSE SENSEX index (S&P Bombay Stock Exchange Sensitive Index) tracks 30 of the largest and most actively traded stocks on the exchange. With a projected GDP growth rate of 7.5 percent in 2015–2016 (The World Bank 2015), the Indian economy could overtake China as the world's fastest-growing economy.

Interestingly, the RBI issues more communications than any other central bank we analyze—on average, more than four times as many as the Fed. This makes them very communicative, but it also makes it difficult to discern the credible signals from chatter. Compounding matters, while lower rates usual correlate with a weaker currency, in India lower interest rates often cause the rupee to rise. Taken together, these idiosyncrasies make RBI communications challenging to decode—but could provide the clearest picture in a cloudy FOREX atmosphere.

To test this assertion, the Reserve Bank of India Index (RBI Index; the solid black line) is set beside two currency pairs in the graph below—the rupee-USD (the broken and dotted line) and the rupee-yuan (the broken line) (Figure 15.11).

The similarities among these data streams are numerous and remarkable. The RBI Index exhibits 10 major and minor peaks

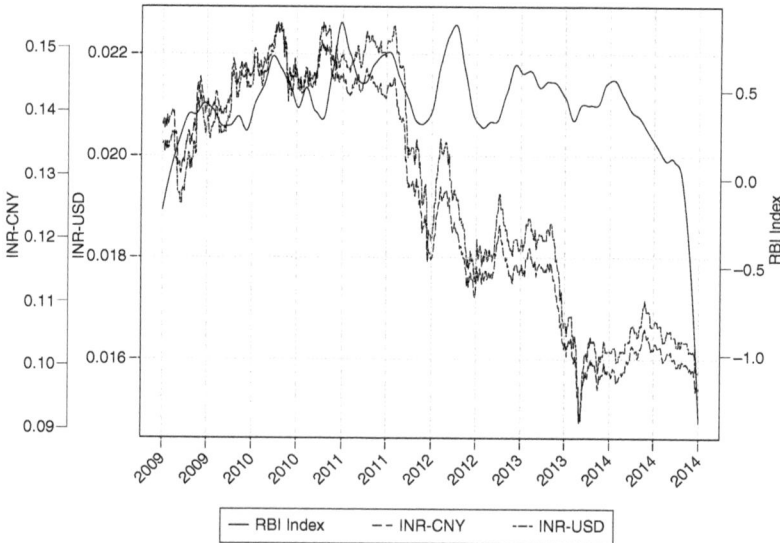

Figure 15.11 RBI Index and exchange rates.

from the beginning of 2009 to the end of 2014, and every one of these peaks finds its analogue in the movements of the currency pairs. From early 2009 to late 2010, for instance, the RBI Index sees three major peaks and both currency pairs manifest these trends. General similarity aside, the first two RBI Index peaks in that stretch—summer 2009 and spring 2010—also anticipate the currency market movements seen in both pairs within a few months. This correlative—and anticipatory—relationship is present throughout the graph, strongly suggesting that the RBI Index could indeed help decode India's convoluted currency fluctuations.

South African Reserve Bank

The South African Reserve Bank (SARB) opened its doors on June 30, 1921 as the result of the South African Parliament's Currency and Banking Act of 1920. The bank's original purpose was to centralize the South African currency and prevent financial loss due to British arbitrage. Before the central bank was established, South African banks issued their own reserve notes and were required to convert those notes to gold on demand. When the price of gold in United Kingdom rose above the price of gold in South Africa, UK traders made a profit by buying gold in South Africa and reselling it in the United Kingdom. The gold had to be repurchased by South African commercial banks at a loss to back their currencies. By centralizing the currency and shifting gold reserves to the reserve bank, the South African Parliament was able to stop losses due to British arbitrage (South African Reserve Bank 2015a).

Headquartered in Pretoria, SARB is a joint-stock company with 2 million shares of capital stock, all of which are privately owned by about 650 individuals. The stock is traded on a over-the-counter facility that is publicly accessible, but which is separate from the Johannesburg Stock Exchange. SARB is governed by a governor, three deputy governors, and eleven directors, all of whom make up the board of directors. Seven of the directors are appointed by the bank's shareholders for three-year terms, while the governor and deputy governors are appointed for five-year terms by the president of the South African Republic. The remaining four directors are appointed by the president for three-year terms (South African Reserve Bank 2015c).

Since its founding, the central bank's powers have expanded. The bank is now responsible for setting interest rates and controlling the liquidity of the money supply to insure price stability, which it defines as inflation from 3 to 6 percent per year. The bank's Monetary Policy Committee, which manipulates policy to fulfill the bank's goals, meets six times per year, or every two months. SARB has made a "commitment to transparent monetary policy" that "has resulted in several initiatives to improve the communication of its policies to the public" (South African Reserve Bank 2015b).

> At the conclusion of every MPC meeting, an MPC statement is issued through a press conference by the Governor of the Bank explaining the reasons for the MPC's policy stance. This press conference is broadcast live on national television and at the same time the MPC statement is released on the Bank's website. (South African Reserve Bank 2015b)

With live, nationally televised broadcasts created to convey monetary policy decisions, the Reserve Bank of South Africa has clearly dedicated itself to open communication with the public.

To assess the relationship between SARB communications and the South African economy, Figure 15.12 places the South African

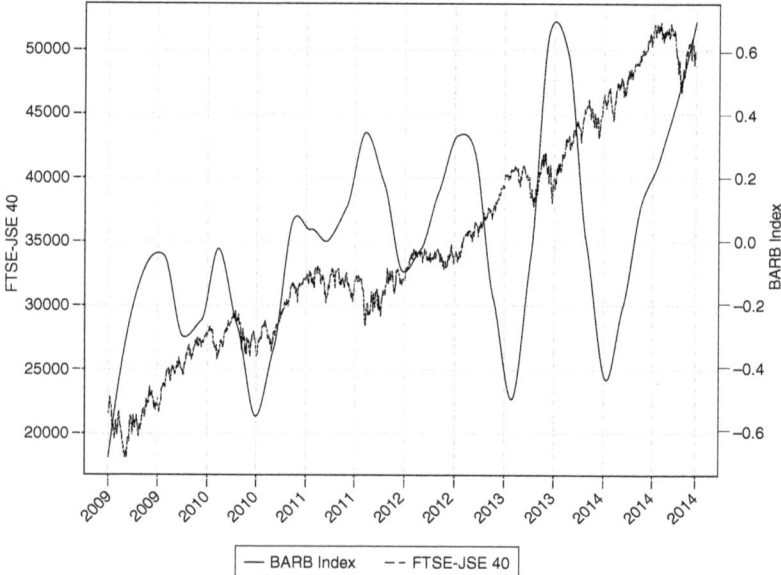

Figure 15.12 SARB Index and FTSE/JSE 40.

Reserve Bank Index (SARB Index) beside the performance of the benchmark equity index (and of, in fact, the entire South African economy): the FTSE/JSE 40.

The SARB Index is represented in Figure 15.12 by the solid black line, and the FTSE-JSE 40 is represented by the broken line. From the end of 2011 to late 2014, the general upward trend in the sentiment indicator matches the market's climb; powerful fluctuations in the Index, however, result in minor movements in the market index. After the SARB Index peaks in the summer of 2012, it descends gratuitously into mild dovish territory before climbing hawkishly again. The equities index mirrors this trend, though at a three- to five-month lag. This analysis mounts a healthy amount of evidence to suggest that there is a strong predictive correlation between the SARB Index and the South African equities market.

* * *

As central banks around the world work to oversee their respective economies, it is clear that open communication has become an integral part of that effort. Often, these dispatches not only relay the sentiments of the central bank from which they come, but they also shape the market that bank oversees—a recent development that makes the impact of these communications consequential for any market actor. Through its unbiased, comprehensive, and quantitative evaluations of these tests, our methodology is able to shed light on the attitudes and influence of central banks worldwide—an influence that spans the equity, the fixed-income, and (especially) the currency markets. Our data also provides students of these institutions and markets a valuable data stream with which to decode international economic developments.

Conclusion

No longer financial black boxes, modern central banks are talkative, even verbose. Of course, this trend is not unilateral—China stands as a marked exception—but the vast majority of these institutions are actively integrating this strategy, and, given recent evidence, it seems likely that the role of open communication in central banking will only continue to expand. For those who study central banks—especially the history of the Fed—this trend is only the latest, logical step in the development of these institutions. It is this sentiment—along with the potential of our analytical methods—that it has been the aim of this book to convey.

By tracing the progress of the Fed from its first days to the financial crisis and beyond, we have attempted to unpack the rationale and circumstances that have brought about the central bank's rise to power and explain that the subsequent adoption of transparency is yet another manifestation of that authority. Along with this narrative, we have presented the Fed's evolution as one story in a growing anthology of analogous developments seen in central banks around the world. By investigating the domestic scene as well as the global picture, we have constructed a comprehensive account of institutional trends and, simultaneously, a formidable foundation for assessment. Through our research we were not only able to identify the rise of transparency as a nearly ubiquitous phenomenon but, also, conclude that our text-based analytical methods are well suited to this development.

* * *

Examining the influence and foresight of central banks through an objective and comprehensive interpretive process that presents its conclusions in quantitative terms, our methodology represents the next, necessary step in the evolution of central bank watching. As we have explored throughout this book, our data is extremely versatile: it can be used to understand fluctuations in the fixed income, equities, and FOREX markets; it can be broken down by correlation to industrial sector or individual equity to shed light on the power central banks have on different assets; it can manage a diverse array of portfolios and achieve significant, market-beating returns. These examples represent only the initial wave of applications for our data, and, as we (and others) continue to study central banks and the markets they move through this method, we can only expect the pool of innovative applications to grow.

Looking forward, we've identified several promising areas of research. Of these, perhaps the most apparent would be an investigation of the market-moving hierarchy of central banks internationally—and the comparative role each bank plays in each market. The communications of key central banks, like the Federal Reserve or the European Central Bank, have significant weight not only in their own economies—but in the global market as well. Understanding the precise level of global influence each central bank commands through communication could significantly contribute to the study of international market trends.

Naturally, this path of research could also lead to better understanding of the fluctuations in individual economies. Because of the domestic and international pull central bank communications have—especially the heavyweight central banks—a comprehensive (and more accurate) understanding of the part these dispatches play in each economy is more complex than an examination of the official central bank of a given nation. Turkey's economic activity, for example, is far more influenced by the ECB than its native central bank, and, consequently, any analysis of the role central banking communications play in this market is manifestly incomplete without taking into account a diversity of institutional voices. Because quantifying the impact of central bank communications is still a young area of study, such multilayered research would represent the frontier of this field.

Another potential direction for continued study would be a deeper investigation of the market expectations that surround these communications. Since central bank watchers project the direction of future communications, market actors that are attentive to these forecasts may adjust their strategies accordingly. Once the actual communication is released, it is quite possible that a gap between the expected central bank sentiment and the actual sentiment could exist. Using our methods, it would be possible to evaluate the score of both the anticipated mood and the actual mood; the difference, should one exist, represents the likelihood of surprise. Advanced knowledge of potential incoming market adjustments would represent an obvious advantage to financial professionals.

This also could lead to an exploration of how the interpretations of central banking communication effect economic change. The market, after all, is influenced not only by central bank texts themselves, but by the analyses of those communications. In its current form, our process produces a score that captures these together: a reaction to a central bank text alone and a reaction to an analysis of a central banking text all fall under the umbrella of the total market reaction. If it were possible to score these separately, it could help identify the accuracy of current analytical methods, help unpack how market actors digest central bank dispatches, and also work toward a deeper understanding of how central banks exert their influence over the economy. This would entail an immensely involved research process—including a specialized implementation of our methodology—but the results could certainly yield worthwhile insight into how monetary policy becomes market movement.

While central banks certainly make waves, economic trends are, of course, the result of many factors. Currently built to evaluate central banking texts, our algorithm could be retooled to assess market-moving data of all stripes. Regulatory bodies, like the Securities and Exchange Commission (SEC), Financial Industry Regulatory Authority (FINRA), and the Commodities Futures Trading Commission (CFTC), also exert influence through their communications, and, utilizing similar processes to that which we developed to examine central banking sentiment, a program customized to these data streams could also be designed and built.

Using our methodology, expansive pieces of regulatory legislation, like Dodd Frank, no longer represent such an interpretive burden. Even seemingly simple legislative directives, like the Volcker Rule, have spawned hundreds or thousands of pages of regulatory rules, and our methods can help shortcut analysis of such complex policy implementation. So, while it may take years and tens of thousands of pages to produce the regulatory rules associated with complex financial legislation, given proper scaling it takes only seconds to analyze that text and clarify complex policy directives.

This potential extends to other forms of regulation and their communication applications. The legal actions of the Food and Drug Administration (FDA) and Environment Protection Agency (EPA), for example, have a substantial impact on food, drug, and energy businesses. To unpack the consequences of regulatory legislation on businesses, lawyers spend countless hours keeping track of the prolific bureaucratic rule-making processes. Leveraging our methodology, we can dramatically reduce such legal efforts. In this arena our data may not be a perfect (or near perfect) substitute for close reading, but it can serve as a reliable and unbiased highlighter, identifying the areas requiring more careful qualitative examination. This simple act could reduce legal costs, speed along regulatory review processes, and democratize the ability to understand and comment on complex government regulations.

The application of this process, however, extends beyond government regulatory and monetary policy bodies—similar variations of our algorithm could be built to assess the communications of private companies as well. By collecting and evaluating shareholder newsletters, press conference texts, meeting transcripts and media reactions to company developments against a lexicon of company specific, reaction-scored words, the effect that current company communications will have on their stock's performance can be better understood—and anticipated. Although the market is already flooded with analysts examining individual equities, our text analysis methods could yield quantitative results that provide ordinal rankings of sentiment toward a stock based on official corporate and regulatory documents. Such data is undeniably more valuable than a simple buy/sell/hold rating. As this and the paragraphs above suggest, the possible applications of this methodology are virtually limitless.

* * *

With so many central banks conversing more than ever before, traditional interpretative techniques, whose detail-centric analysis already limits credibility, will only seem all the more conspicuously restricted. In other words, the assessments (and forecasts) derived from a small sampling of specific words and phrases—orthodox central bank watching—necessarily become less representative of central banking sentiment as the data set from which they were pulled grows in size. To maintain its relevance, central bank watching needs an inclusive interpretive methodology, and this book has presented a novel method of central banking analysis built from the ground up to be inclusive.

This inclusivity leverages the comprehensive approach that has marked the recent wave of "Big Data" applications, while, at the same time, being grounded in domain expertise. The financial technology world is flooded with firms using simplified text analysis techniques to glean the sentiment out of social networks, blogs, news, and almost any other form of text. The trouble is that most of these firms rely on set dictionaries of terms, some are dubbed positive, some negative, and the sentiment is calculated by adding positive buzzwords together then subtracting out the negative buzzwords. There are many variations of this simple method, but all rely on building (often complex) dictionaries of terms or phrases and presuming that language does not evolve faster than the established word bank. Unfortunately for the computer scientists reliant on this methodology, complex market dynamics and corresponding policy issues tend to evolve quickly—and often with their own lexicon.

What are less common—and more vital—are applications that harness domain expertise to help unlock the potential of the wealth of data now available. Domain experts can not only train a system to evolve with changing linguistic cues, but their analysis relies on a logical combination of individual words and the content in which those words are communicated. When this type of domain expertise is added to text analytics methods utilizing impartial scaling and coupled with a sufficiently large amount of data (text), the end result is valuable, comprehensive, unbiased, quantitative data.

Essentially, data science alone cannot develop valuable data on complex subjects like central banking or regulation without domain experts providing viable parameters to reduce the nearly infinite number of dimensions upon which language can be scaled. Thus, it is necessary to have a combination of deep domain expertise and valuable methodological skills to accurately analyze central bank (and all other complex) communications. That is why our firm understanding of the history of central banking institutions, the markets in which they operate, and our grasp of economics, statistics, and computer science methodology has given us the foundation necessary to build intelligent and informed interpretive programs. These are programs that not only point out interesting patterns in colossal data sets, but sort through the noise and clutter of central bank communications to provide efficient, expert assessments as well.

As was briefly mentioned above, this approach has broad applications within, and beyond, financial data. Human beings, and especially their institutions, are never at a loss for words, and these words are data. Our methodology not only treats words as data, but whole communications as data sets requiring expertise to properly scale, score, and examine. There are numerous institutions, private and public, whose voices impact market developments and, therefore, could be understood more thoroughly through a specialized application of our methodology. We chose central banks first because of our specific expertise and because of the influence central banks wield, but we look forward to what further research will reveal about the remaining of gears of the financial machine.

Ultimately, this book isn't only about offering a different way of understanding the influence of central banks; it's about a different way of understanding the entire market. Vast sets of data sit relatively unused, and our work serves as an initial effort toward unlocking the potential buried in the strong, rapid current of communication that drives market dynamics. We believe that the forefront of financial data is a marriage between domain expertise and data processing technology. We believe that the future of finance lies hidden in plain sight—a puzzle in the prattle.

Bibliography

Armerding, Taylor. *Big data without good analytics can lead to bad decisions.* August 26, 2013. http://www.infoworld.com/article/2611729/big-data/big-data-without-good-analytics-can-lead-to-bad-decisions.html (accessed May 15, 2015).

Axilrod, Stephen. *Inside the Fed: Monetary Policy and Its Management, Martin through Greenspan to Bernanke.* MIT Press, 2011a.

Axilrod, Stephen, interview by Evan Schnidman. *Interview on the U.S. Federal Reserve Bank.* November 23, 2011b.

Bailey, Andrew and Cheryl Schonhardt-Bailey. "Does Deliberation Matter in FOMC Monetary Policymaking?: The Volcker Revolution of 1979." *Political Analysis* 16.4 (2008): 404–427.

Bank of Canada. *About the Bank.* 2015a. http://www.bankofcanada.ca/about/ (accessed May 15, 2015).

———. *The Bank's History.* 2015b. http://www.bankofcanada.ca/about/history/ (accessed May 15, 2015).

Bank of England. *About the Bank.* 2015. http://www.bankofengland.co.uk/about/Pages/default.aspx (accessed May 2015, 2015).

Bank of Israel. *About the Bank of Israel.* 2015. http://www.bankisrael.gov.il/en/Pages/Default.aspx (accessed May 15, 2015).

Bank of Japan. *Outline of the Bank.* 2015. http://www.boj.or.jp/en/about/outline/index.htm (accessed May 15, 2015).

Bank of Korea. *About Bank of Korea.* 2015. http://eng.bok.or.kr/broadcast.action?menuNaviId=792 (accessed May 15, 2015).

Bank of Mexico. *About Banco de México.* 2015a. http://www.banxico.org.mx/acerca-del-banco-de-mexico/about-banco-mexico-.html (accessed May 15, 2015).

———. *Board of Governors.* 2015b. http://www.banxico.org.mx/acerca-del-banco-de-mexico/board-of-governors.html (accessed May 15, 2015).

Bank of Russia. *Bank of Russia.* 2015a. http://www.cbr.ru/eng/ (accessed May 15, 2015).

———. *Board of Directors.* 2015b. http://www.cbr.ru/Eng/today/?PrtId=dir (accessed May 15, 2015).

———. *Legal Status and Functions of the Bank of Russia.* 2015c. http://www.cbr.ru/eng/today/?Prtid=bankstatus (accessed May 15, 2015).

Bensel, Richard Franklin. *Yankee Leviathan: The Origins of Central State Authority in America*. Cambridge, England; New York: Cambridge University Press, 1991.

Binder, Sarah and Mark Spindel. "Monetary Politics: Origins of the Federal Reserve." *Studies in American Political Development* 27.01 (April 2013): 1–13.

Blackstone, Brian. *Central Banks Move to Drive Down Currencies, Yielding Domino Effect*. February 9, 2015. http://www.wsj.com/articles/central-banks-move-to-drive-down-currencies-yielding-domino-effect-1423421248 (accessed May 15, 2015).

Blinder, Alan S., Charles Goodhart, Philipp Hildebrand, David Lipton, and Charles Wyplosz. *How Do Central Banks Talk?: Geneva Reports on the World Economy 3*. Geneva; London: Centre for Economic Policy Research, 2001.

Board of Governors of the Federal Reserve System. "Annual Report Covering Operations for Year 1947." Technical Report, Washington, DC, 1948.

Board of Governors of the Federal Reserve System. "Federal Reserve Bulletin." Technical Report, Washington, DC, 1949, 776.

———. *Frequently Asked Questions*. April 2015a. http://www.federalreserve.gov/faqs/money_19277.htm (accessed May 15, 2015).

———. *Press Release*. January 9, 2015b. http://www.federalreserve.gov/newsevents/press/other/20150109a.htm (accessed May 15, 2015).

———. *The Economists*. 2015c. http://www.federalreserve.gov/econresdata/theeconomists.htm (accessed May 15, 2015).

Bremner, Robert P. *Chairman of the Fed: William McChesney Martin Jr. and the Creation of the Modern American Financial System*. Yale University Press, 2004.

Brook, Anne-Marie, Frank Sedillot, and Patrice Ollivaud. *Channels for Narrowing the US Current Account Deficit and Implications for Other Economies—Papers—OECD iLibrary*. May 2004. http://www.oecd-ilibrary.org/economics/channels-for-narrowing-the-us-current-account-deficit-and-implications-for-other-economies_263550547141;jsessionid=ea5bv1k8qh22.x-oecd-live-02 (accessed May 15, 2015).

Bruner, Robert F. and Sean D. Carr. *The Panic of 1907: Lessons Learned from the Market's Perfect Storm*. Hoboken, NJ: Wiley, 2009.

Buttonwood. *The ECB and QE: The Day after Textbar The Economist*. January 23, 2015. http://www.economist.com/blogs/buttonwood/2015/01/ecb-and-qe (accessed May 15, 2015).

Casey, Theo. *The 'Fed Model' Is Warning Us to be Careful*. April 28, 2010. http://moneyweek.com/investment-strategy-fed-model-of-stock-valuation-01708/ (accessed May 15, 2015).

Central Bank of Brazil. *History*. 2015a. http://www.bcb.gov.br/?HISTORY (accessed May 15, 2015).

———. *National Monetary Council: Secretariat*. 2015b. http://www.bcb.gov.br/?CMNEN (accessed May 2015, 2015).

Centre Virtuel de la Connaissance sur l'Europe. *The Third Stage of Economic and Monetary Union*. November 9, 2012. http://www.cvce.eu/obj/the_third_stage_of_Economic_and_monetary_union-en-e2e91dc0-3a6d-49fc-b3f8-f96fb5f3addb.html (accessed May 2015, 15).

Congressional Research Service. "Memo to the Senate Energy and Natural Resources Committee: Export-Import Bank Financing of Liquefied Natural Gas-Related Transactions." Congressional Committee Report, Congressional Research Service, 2013.

Council of Economic Advisers. "The Economic Report of the President." 1953.

Crosse, Gary and Jan Paschal. *Timeline: Federal Reserve's Transparency Steps.* January 25, 2012. http://www.reuters.com/article/2012/01/25/us-usa-fed-communications-idUSTRE80O2QQ20120125 (accessed May 15, 2015).

Dawnay, Kim. *A History of Sterling.* October 8, 2001. http://www.telegraph.co.uk/news/1399693/A-history-of-sterling.html (accessed May 15, 2015).

Deutsche Bundesbank. *Understanding the Capital Key.* January 16, 2014. https://www.bundesbank.de/Redaktion/EN/Topics/2014/2014_01_16_understanding_the_capital_key.html (accessed May 15, 2015).

Dillon, Douglas. "Memorandum for the President McChesney." Memorandum, Martin Collection, Missouri Historical Society, 1964.

Dominguez, Kathryn M. "Central Bank Intervention and Exchange Rate Volatility1." *Journal of International Money and Finance* 17.1 (February 1998): 161–190.

Draghi, Mario. "ECB: Introductory statement to the plenary debate of the European Parliament on the ECB's Annual Report 2013." *ECB: Introductory Statement to the Plenary Debate of the European Parliament on the ECB's Annual Report 2013.* February 25, 2015.

Eccles, Marriner S. "Summary of Meeting of President Truman and the Federal Open Market Committee." Notes, 1951.

Economists' National Committee On Monetary Policy. "Press Release: 51 Members Urge the Importance of Restoring and Maintaining the Independence of the Federal Reserve System." 1951.

Economy Watch. *The Australian Economy.* March 9, 2010. http://www.economywatch.com/world_Economy/australia (accessed May 15, 2015).

Ehrmann, Michael and Marcel Fratzscher. "Communication by Central Bank Committee Members: Different Strategies, Same Effectiveness?" *Journal of Money, Credit and Banking* 39.2–3 (March 2007): 509–541.

European Central Bank. *Economic and Monetary Union (EMU).* 2015a. http://www.ecb.europa.eu/ecb/history/emu/html/index.en.html (accessed May 15, 2015).

———. *Open Market Operations.* 2015b. https://www.ecb.europa.eu/mopo/implement/omo/html/index.en.html (accessed May 15, 2015).

European Central Bank. "The ECB's Response to the Financial Crisis." *Monthly Bulletin*, October, 2010.

European Commission. *Economic and Financial Affairs.* 2015. http://ec.europa.eu/economy_finance/euro/why/index_En.htm (accessed May 2014, 2015).

European Union. *Eurostat News Release.* May 20, 2015. http://ec.europa.eu/eurostat/documents/2995521/6836772/6-20052015-BP-EN.pdf/1b8e0bd3-a47d-4ef4-bca6-9fbb7ef1c7f9 (accessed May 27, 2015).

Federal Open Market Committee. *Transcripts and Other Historical Materials.* 2012. http://www.federalreserve.gov/monetarypolicy/fomc_historical.htm (accessed May 15, 2015).

Financial Times. *Abenomics Definition*. 2015a. http://lexicon.ft.com/Term?term=abenomics (accessed May 15, 2015).

———. *Financial Policy Committee Definition*. 2015b. http://lexicon.ft.com/Term?term=Financial-Policy-Committee--FPC (accessed May 15, 2015).

Flaherty, Edward. *A Brief History of Central Banking in the United States*. 2010. http://odur.let.rug.nl/~usa/E/usbank/bankxx.htm (accessed May 15, 2015).

Fratzscher, Marcel. "Communication and Exchange Rate Policy." *Journal of Macroeconomics* 30.4 (December 2008): 1651–1672.

Glennerster, Herbert, Rachel M'cleod, and Tavneet Suri. *How Bad Data Fed the Ebola Epidemic*. January 30, 2015. http://www.nytimes.com/2015/01/31/opinion/how-bad-data-fed-the-ebola-epidemic.html (accessed May 15, 2015).

Hately, James. "The 'Maple Bond' Market." Financial System Review, Bank of Canada, 2012.

Heath, Michael. *Australia Opens China's Services Market with Free Trade Accord*. November 17, 2014. http://www.bloomberg.com/news/articles/2014-11-17/australia-china-to-sign-free-trade-deal-spurring-economic-shift (accessed May 15, 2015).

Holmes, Anne. *Australia's Economic Relationships with China*. 2015. http://www.aph.gov.au/About_Parliament/Parliamentary_Departments/Parliamentary_Library/pubs/BriefingBook44p/China (accessed May 15, 2015).

Holmes, Douglas. *The Economy of Words*. Chicago, IL: U of Chicago Press, 2013.

Institute for Monetary and Economic Studies of the Bank of Japan. *Organization and Management of the Bank*. White Paper, Bank of Japan, 2004.

Ishiguro, Rie and Shinji Kitamura. *Japan Quake's Economic Impact Worse than First Feared Textbar*. April 12, 2011. http://www.reuters.com/article/2011/04/12/japan-economy-idUSL3E7FC09220110412 (accessed May 15, 2015).

Joint Committee on the Economic Report. "Money, Credit and Fiscal Policies." 1950.

Joint Committee on the Economic Report. "Report of the Joint Committee on the Economic Report." 1952.

Joint Committee on the Economic Report. "Report of the Joint Committee on the Economic Report." 1954.

Jordan, Thomas. *Speech by Thomas Jordan, Vice Chair*. September 28, 2011. http://www.snb.ch/en/mmr/speeches/id/ref_20110928_tjn/source/ref_20110928_tjn.en.pdf (accessed May 15, 2015).

Kim, Christine and Choonsik Yoo. *South Korea Could Keep Expansionary Policy for Years Textbar Reuters*. September 16, 2014. http://www.reuters.com/article/2014/09/16/us-southkorea-economy-cenbank-idUSKBN0HB00520140916 (accessed May 15, 2015).

Kim, Suk-Joong and Jeffrey Sheen. "The Determinants of Foreign Exchange Intervention by Central Banks: Evidence from Australia." *Journal of International Money and Finance* 21.5 (October 2002): 619–649.

Knipe, James. "Office Correspondence: Paper on Public Criticism of the Federal Reserve System." Correspondence, William McChesney Martin Jr. Collection. Missouri Historical Society, 1962.

Knott, Jack H. "The Fed Chairman as a Political Executive." *Administration & Society* 18.2 (August 1986): 197–231.

Lanston, Aubrey. "The Treasury-Federal Reserve Dispute." *The Treasury-Federal Reserve Dispute*. Pennsylvania Bankers Association, February 1951.

Law Librarians Society of Washington, DC. *The Federal Reserve Act of 1913: A Legislative History*. September 2014. http://www.llsdc.org/FRA-LH (accessed May 15, 2015).

Leonard, David and Peter Coy. *Alan Greenspan on His Fed Legacy and the Economy*. August 9, 2012. http://www.bloomberg.com/bw/articles/2012-08-09/alan-greenspan-on-his-fed-legacy-and-the-economy (accessed May 15, 2015).

Marsh, David. *Dangers of Central Banks' Public Investments*. June 15, 2014. http://www.usatoday.com/story/money/markets/2014/06/15/david-marsh-new-force-in-world-markets-global-public-investors/10548183/ (accessed May 15, 2015).

Martin, William McChesney. "Annual Report of the Board of Governors of the Federal Reserve System: Covering the Operations of the Year 1952." Technical Report, Board of Governors of the Federal Reserve System, 1953.

McCabe, Thomas. "Letter to President Truman." *Letter to President Truman*. February 7, 1951a.

———. "Letter to Treasury Secretary Snyder." February 7, 1951b.

Meltzer, Allan. *A History of the Federal Reserve, Volume 1: 1913–1951*. University of Chicago Press, 2003.

Meltzer, Allan. "Politics and the Fed." *Journal of Monetary Economics* July 2010: 39–48.

Moss, David A. and Cole Bolton. *The Federal Reserve and the Banking Crisis of 1931*. January 2009. http://www.hbs.edu/faculty/Pages/item.aspx?num=36824.

Mundy, Simon and Song Jung-a. *Bank of Korea Calls for Fiscal Measures to Stimulate Economy*. April 9, 2015. http://www.ft.com/cms/s/0/f2f4dc32-de71-11e4-ba43-00144feab7de.html#axzz3ZCM7uFGV (accessed May 15, 2015).

Nissan, Yossi. *Bank of Israel Buys $400m in Foreign Currency*. April 29, 2015. http://www.globes.co.il/en/article-bank-of-israel-buys-400m-in-foreign-currency-1001031600 (accessed May 15, 2015).

Nixon, Simon. *QE Is Working Better Than ECB Dared Hope*. April 15, 2015. http://www.wsj.com/articles/suddenly-qe-becomes-flavor-of-the-month-for-the-eurozone-1429129592 (accessed May 15, 2015).

Observatory of Economic Complexity. *OEC: Australia Profile of Exports, Imports and Trade Partners*. 2015. https://atlas.media.mit.edu/en/profile/country/aus/ (accessed May 2015, 2015).

Peters, Will. *GBP/EUR Forecasts for 2015 Warns Pound Now Overvalued*. November 16, 2014. https://www.poundsterlinglive.com/exchange-rate-forecasts/1748-november-s-pound-euro-exchange-rate-forecasts-for-period-2014-2015 (accessed May 15, 2015).

Rendall, Alasdair. *Economic Terms Explained*. November 12, 2007. http://news.bbc.co.uk/2/hi/programmes/bbc_parliament/7090665.stm (accessed May 15, 2015).

Reserve Bank of Australia. *RBA: A Brief History*. 2015. http://www.rba.gov.au/about-rba/history/index.html (accessed May 15, 2015).

Reserve Bank of India. *Organisation*. 2015a. https://www.rbi.org.in/Scripts/AboutUsDisplay.aspx?pg=OrganizationStructure.htm (accessed May 15, 2015).

———. *Projects*. 2015b. https://www.rbi.org.in/Scripts/Project1.aspx (accessed May 15, 2015).

Reserve Bank of New Zealand. *About Us*. 2015. http://www.rbnz.govt.nz/about_us/ (accessed May 15, 2015).

Robinson, Blaise. *European Stock Markets Cheer ECB QE Textbar Reuters*. January 22, 2015. http://www.reuters.com/article/2015/01/22/markets-stocks-europe-idUSL6N0V14OG20150122 (accessed May 2015).

Schnidman, Evan. *Fed Inflation Goal Is More Politics Than Policy*. February 5, 2012. http://www.bloomberg.com/news/articles/2012-02-06/fed-inflation-goal-is-more-politics-than-policy-evan-schnidman (accessed May 26, 2015).

Slavin, Kevin, interview by Guy Raz. "Should We Be Wary of Algorithms?" *TED Radio Hour*. National Public Radio, Washington. March 6, 2015.

South African Reserve Bank. *History*. 2015a. https://www.resbank.co.za/AboutUs/History/Pages/History-Home.aspx (accessed May 15, 2015).

———. *Monetary Policy*. 2015b. https://www.resbank.co.za/MonetaryPolicy/Pages/MonetaryPolicy-Home.aspx (accessed May 15, 2015).

———. *Structure*. 2015c. https://www.resbank.co.za/AboutUs/Structure/Pages/Structure-Home.aspx (accessed May 15, 2015).

Stein, Jeremy. "Evaluating Large-Scale Asset Purchases." *Evaluating Large-Scale Asset Purchases*. Brookings Institution, Washington, DC, October 11, 2012.

Stewart, James. *Wondering What the Fed's Statements Mean? Be Patient*. March 13, 2015. http://www.nytimes.com/2015/03/13/business/still-reading-the-feds-tea-leaves-word-by-word.html (accessed May 2015, 2015).

Stockwell, Eleanor. "Working at the Board 1930s–1970s." *Working at the Board 1930s-1970s*. FRASER Electronic Records: Federal Reserve Bank of St. Louis, 1989.

Sveriges Riksbank. *Organisation*. 2015a. http://www.riksbank.se/en/The-Riksbank/Organisation/ (accessed May 15, 2015).

———. *The Tasks and Role of the Riksbank*. 2015b. http://www.riksbank.se/en/The-Riksbank/The-Riksbanks-role-in-the-economy/ (accessed May 15, 2015).

Swiss National Bank. *The SNB*. 2015. http://www.snb.ch/en/iabout/snb (accessed May 15, 2015).

"The Bank of Japan Act." 2007.

The Economist. *The Economist Explains: Why China's Economy Is Slowing*. March 11, 2015. http://www.economist.com/blogs/economist-explains/2015/03/economist-explains-8 (accessed May 15, 2015).

The Federal Reserve Bank of Minneapolis. *A History of Central Banking in the United States*. 2015. https://www.minneapolisfed.org/community/student-resources/central-bank-history/history-of-central-banking (accessed May 15, 2015).

The World Bank. *Global Economic Prospects: Forecast Table.* 2015. https://www.worldbank.org/en/publication/global-economic-prospects/summary-table (accessed May 15, 2015).

US Census Bureau. "Census Bureau Projects U.S. and World Populations on New Year's Day." Press Release, 2014.

US Treasury Department. "Annual Report of the Secretary of the Treasury on the State of the Finances For the Fiscal Year Ended June 30, 1953." Technical Report, 1954.

United States Treasury and Federal Reserve Board of Governors. "Joint Announcement by the Secretary of The Treasury and the Chairman of the Board of Governors, and of the Federal Open Market Committee, of the Federal Reserve System." Press Release, 1951.

Vayid, Ianthi. "Central Bank Communications Before, During and After the Crisis: From Open-Market Operations to Open-Mouth Policy." Working Paper, Bank of Canada, 2013.

Volker, Paul. "Remarks at the 1984 Cosmos Club Award." *Remarks at the 1984 Cosmos Club Award.* Washington, DC, May 1984.

Warsh, Kevin. "Transparency and the Bank of England's Monetary Policy Committee." Bank of England, 2014.

Wells, Donald R. *The Federal Reserve System: A History.* Jefferson, NC: McFarland, 2004.

Wicker, Elmus R. "The World War II Policy of Fixing a Pattern of Interest Rates." *The Journal of Finance* 24.3 (June 1969): 447–458.

Wilson, Thomas Frederick. *The Power "to Coin" Money: The Exercise of Monetary Powers by the Congress.* M.E. Sharpe, 1992.

Woolley, John T. *Monetary Politics: The Federal Reserve and the Politics of Monetary Policy.* Cambridge: Cambridge University Press, 1986.

Yellen, Janet. "Revolution and Evolution in Central Bank Communications." Haas School of Business, University of California, Berkeley, Berkeley, California, November 13, 2012.

———. "Communication in Monetary Policy." Washington, DC, April 4, 2013.

Index

1951 Accord, 25–30

Aldrich Plan, 10–11, 23
algorithm
    Prattle, 62, 185–6
    Wall Street, 65–6
Axilrod, Stephen, 32, 41, 43–6

backtest
    equity markets, 88
    fixed-income markets, 69, 71–5
    forecast, 93–4, 97
Beige Book, 47
Bernanke, Ben, 55, 58
Binder, Sarah, 12–13
Blue Book, 38
Bretton Woods, 20, 40, 128
Brill, Daniel, 35, 37
Burns, Arthur, 39–41, 44, 52, 54
buzzwords, 62–3, 187

Carter, Jimmy, 44
centralization, of the Fed, 4, 9, 15–16, 31, 38
close reading
    legal, 186
    literary, 56, 59
Committee on Interests and Dividends (CID), 40
commodities
    Australian, 150, 152
    Commodities Futures Trading Commission (CFTC), 185
    markets, 157

Dodd Frank, 185
domain expertise, 61, 63, 187–8
Douglas, Paul, 22–3, 25–6
Draghi, Mario, 118, 121

Eccles, Marriner, 21, 23–4
Eisenhower, Dwight D., 28–9
Environment Protection Agency (EPA), 186
European Commission, 116–17
European Union (EU), 116–18, 120–2
exchange rate, 56, 99–102, 111, 167
exchange-traded fund (ETF), 71

Fed watching, 2–3, 54, 57, 59, 60, 63–5, 92
Federal Deposit Insurance Corporation (FDIC), 18
federal funds rate (FFR), 69, 75–6
Federal Reserve Reform Act of 1977, 43
financial crisis, 57, 74, 75, 82, 84, 98, 120
Financial Industry Regulatory Authority (FINRA), 185
Food and Drug Administration (FDA), 186
Fratzscher, Marcel, 79, 81–2, 99, 101–2
Freedom of Information Act, 36, 41

Great Depression, 16–17, 51, 160, 164
Green Book, 38
Greenspan, Alan, 2, 4, 48, 52–5

innovation
  approach, 157, 184
  policy, 44–5, 53
investment models, 66–7, 74–7

Knipe, James, 32–3
Korean War, 23, 25, 28

long-term refinancing operation (LTRO), 119

M2, 40
main refinancing operation (MRO), 119–20
market
  currency, 99–111, 144–5, 156–7, 165–6, 178–9
  equity, 77, 79–89, 110–11, 124–5, 133–5, 141–4, 151–4, 161–2, 167–9, 172, 174–6, 178, 181, 184
  fixed income, 77, 79, 80, 83–4, 97, 111, 122–3, 143–5, 152–4, 160, 162–4, 170–1, 181
Martin, William McChesney, 26–8, 31–3, 39, 45, 51

New Deal, 17–18
Nixon, Richard, 31, 39–40

paper trading, full, 71–2
Patman, Wright, 34–5
portfolio
  control, 74, 135–6
  Fed Index, 69, 74–5, 77, 87–8, 97–8, 135–6, 184

position
  long, 71–2, 87, 97–8, 136
  short, 71–2, 136
Proxmire, William, 34–5

qualitative evaluations, 3, 59, 64–7
quantitative
  easing, 120, 131–2, 140
  evaluations, 3, 61–2, 64–5, 125

rational expectations philosophy, 54
regional banks, 32, 36–8, 47–8
Reserve Bank Operating Committee (RBOC), 11–14

Securities and Exchange Commission (SEC), 18, 185
selection bias, 62–3
sentiment analysis
  Prattle, 62–3, 116, 125
  traditional, 62–3
Snyder, John, 23–4
Spindel, Mark, 12–13
Sproul, Alan, 23

track changes, 57
Treasury, the United States, 10, 16–29, 47
Truman, Harry S., 19–21, 24, 26–8

Volcker, Paul, 4, 44–7, 51–2
Volcker Rule, 185

Yellen, Janet, 4, 55, 58

Printed in the USA
CPSIA information can be obtained
at www.ICGtesting.com
LVHW011610240824
789147LV00002B/84